Delaware

Digest of Laws relating to Free Schools in the State of

Delaware

Delaware

Digest of Laws relating to Free Schools in the State of Delaware

ISBN/EAN: 9783337187781

Printed in Europe, USA, Canada, Australia, Japan

Cover: Foto ©ninafisch / pixelio.de

More available books at **www.hansebooks.com**

DIGEST OF LAWS

RELATING TO

FREE SCHOOLS

IN THE

STATE OF DELAWARE.

PUBLISHED BY AUTHORITY OF SECTION 10, CHAPTER 369,

VOLUME 16, LAWS OF DELAWARE.

1881:

JAMES KIRK & SONS, PRINTERS,

DOVER, DELAWARE.

SCHOOL LAWS OF DELAWARE.

ARTICLE I.

SUPERINTENDENT.

On the second Tuesday in April, annually, the Governor shall ap- Sec. 1, Chap. 46, Vol. 16.
point and commission some suitable person, of good moral character, State Superin-
and well qualified in regard to his mental attainments for the place, tendent to be appointed.
as Superintendent of the Free Schools of the State of Delaware, who Qualifications.
shall hold his office for one year and until his successor shall in like Term of office.
manner be appointed. The Governor shall have power to fill any Vacancy.
vacancy caused by death, resignation, or otherwise.

The Superintendent shall visit every school once a year. He shall Sec. 4, Chap. 46, Vol. 16.
note in a book, to be kept for that purpose, the number of scholars; Duties of State Superintendent.
the condition of school building, ground and appurtenances; the
qualification and efficiency of the teachers; the conduct and standing
of the scholars; the method of instruction, and the discipline and
government of the schools. In the visits of the Superintendent to the
schools, he shall advise with the teachers respectively, and give them
such instructions in regard to discipline and teaching as he may deem
necessary, and shall have power to suspend or withdraw any teacher's When he may withdraw
certificate upon his refusal to comply with the reasonable directions of certificates.
the Superintendent, subject, however, to an appeal, as in other cases.
He shall, by every means in his power, strive to promote and advance
the cause of education and interest in the schools, and, in order to
secure his entire time, he shall not engage in any other business, or Shall engage in no other business.
pursue any other calling.

The Superintendent shall examine all persons who shall apply to Sec. 5, Chap. 46, Vol. 16.
him for that purpose, and who propose to teach in this State, and any Who shall be examined.
one interested may attend such examination, which may be oral, or by

Mode of examination.

Where and when held.

Who shall be recommended for a first grade certificate.

printed or written questions, or partly by each method. These examinations may be at such times and places as the Superintendent may appoint, having due regard to the necessities of the schools and the convenience of the teachers. Every applicant who is of good moral character, and who shall be found qualified to teach orthography, reading, writing, mental arithmetic, written arithmetic, geography, history of the United States, English grammar, elements of rhetoric, algebra, geometry, and natural philosophy, shall be recommended to the State Board of Education for a first grade certificate ; and the said

When certificate shall issue.

How signed.

Good for how long.

Board, approving the same, shall authorize and direct such certificate to issue, signed by the Superintendent, and countersigned by the President of said Board, and the certificate so issued shall be good for three years, unless sooner revoked by the Superintendent for cause, to

Who shall receive second grade certificate.

be approved by said Board. Every applicant who is of good moral character, and who shall, in examination, answer ninety *per centum* of all questions asked in orthography, reading, writing, mental arithmetic, written arithmetic, geography, history of the United States, and English grammar, shall receive, from the Superintendent, a second

How long good.

grade certificate, which shall be good for two years, unless sooner revoked for cause, to be approved by said Board. If any such ap-

Who shall receive third grade certificate.

plicant fail to answer ninety *per centum* of the questions asked in examination, in the branches mentioned for a second grade certificate, but shall answer at least sixty *per centum* thereof, he shall receive from the Superintendent a third grade certificate, which shall be good for

How long good.

one year, unless sooner revoked for cause. Any applicant having

Who may appeal.

been refused a certificate may appeal to the State Board of Education.

Superintendent shall keep list of certificates.

Chap. 355, Vol. 16.

The Superintendent shall also keep an accurate list of all certificates granted by him, with the dates thereof, and the names of the persons to whom granted.

Sec. 6, Chap. 46, Vol. 16.

Section 4, Chap. 369, Vol. 16.

Salary $1,500. How drawn.

The State Superintendent shall receive a salary of fifteen hundred dollars per annum, to be paid quarterly by the State Treasurer on warrants drawn by himself and marked correct by the State Auditor ; but the State Auditor shall not mark such warrant correct when such Superintendent has failed to discharge his duties faithfully and to the best of his abilities.

Sec. 7, Chap. 46, Vol. 16.

The State Superintendent shall annually, on the first Tuesday in

December, in each and every year, report in writing to the Governor *Annual report to the Governor.* the condition of the public schools, and make such recommendations and suggestions as he may think proper.

The Superintendent shall hold a teachers' institute, in each of the *Sec. 11, Chap. 46, Vol. 16.* counties of this State, at least once a year, of at least three days' *Teachers' Institute.* session, at which time all the teachers in their respective counties shall *When held.* attend, unless unavoidably detained; at which time the Superintendent *Duties of Teachers.* shall give all the information to teachers within his power, and such *Duties of Superintendent.* other instructions as he may deem advisable for the advancement of education, and have a general interchange of views of teachers as to the wants of the various schools.

The Superintendent shall, by the consent of the State Board of *Sec. 13, Chap. 46, Vol. 16.* Education, or a majority of them, have power to re-district, or *When Superintendent may* consolidate, any of the districts in Sussex County, when, in his judg- *re-district, or consolidate, any* ment, such consolidation or re-districting is necessary for the promo- *district in Sussex county.* tion of education in said county; *provided, however*, he shall not interfere with any consolidated district or incorporated board of education.

The Superintendent shall purchase all the school books used in the *Sec. 5, Chap. 369, Vol. 16.* public schools of the State, at the lowest price at which the same can *Superintendent to purchase* be obtained, first inviting competition, and draw his warrant upon the *school books.* State Treasurer for the amount thereof in favor of the person supplying *How paid for.* the same, which he is hereby authorized to pay. The Superintend- *Distribution of school books.* ent shall also distribute said books at the price at which they were purchased to the clerk of each school district in this State, as said clerk may indicate upon his written order for the same. He shall also pay over to the State Treasurer, quarterly, the money received from the clerks of the several school districts for school books, as herein- after provided for, and also at the same time furnish the State Treasurer a list of the school books, and their respective prices, supplied to each *List of school books, to whom* clerk of the district during the preceding three months. The State *rendered.* Superintendent, before entering upon the duties of his office, shall give *Bond of superintendent.* bond to the State of Delaware, with at least three sureties, to be ap- proved by the Governor, in the penalty of fifteen thousand dollars, with conditions as follows, viz: The condition of the above obligation *Condition.* is such, that if the above named ———— ————, being State Superintendent, shall and do well and truly account for all money which shall come to his hands from the several school districts of this State, and shall pay and apply the same according to law, and deliver to his successor in office all school books on hand at the expiration of his term of office, then the above written obligation shall be void. To the said

Warrant of Attorney. bond there shall be subjoined a warrant of attorney to confess judgment thereon, and the said bond and warrant of attorney shall be joint and several.

Sec. 7, Chap. 369, Vol. 16. Record of Superintendent. The Superintendent shall keep a book, in which shall be recorded in the proper form all his acts and doings with reference to the purchase and distribution of books as hereinbefore provided. The clerk of each school district shall also keep a record of the school books received and distributed, and also the amount received therefor, in an itemized form.

ARTICLE II.

ASSISTANT SUPERINTENDENT.

Sec. 1, Chap. 369, Vol. 16. Appointment of Assistant Superintendent. The Governor, at the time of the appointment of the State Superintendent, shall appoint and commission some suitable person as Assistant Superintendent of the Free Schools of the State of Delaware, who shall hold his office for the term of one year and until his successor shall be appointed.

Sec. 3, Chap. 369, Vol. 16. Duties of Assistant Superintendent. It shall be the duty of the Assistant Superintendent to aid the State Superintendent in the performance of his duties now imposed by law, and to that end shall be subject to his direction. It shall also be the

Secretary. duty of the Assistant Superintendent to act as Secretary of the State Board of Education.

Sec. 4, Chap. 369, Vol. 16. He shall receive a salary of eight hundred dollars per annum as compensation for all the duties herein imposed upon him, to be paid in the same manner as the salary of the State Superintendent is now paid.

ARTICLE III.

STATE BOARD OF EDUCATION.

Sec. 2, Chap. 369, Vol. 16. State Board of Education. The Secretary of State, President of Delaware College, and the State Superintendent, shall constitute a State Board of Education for this State, who shall meet on the first Tuesday of January, in each and every year, in the Capitol, at Dover, at 2 o'clock in the afternoon. The Assistant Superintendent shall act as Secretary of said Board of Education. The President of Delaware College shall, by virtue of his office, be President of said Board of Education. The State Board of Education shall hear appeals and determine finally all matters of controversy between the Superintendent and teachers or commissioners, and between school commissioners and teachers; the State Board of Education, together with the State Superintendent, shall determine what text books are to be used in the free schools of this State. The State Board of Education, together with the State Superintendent, shall issue an uniform series of blanks for the use of teachers, and shall require all records to be kept and returns to be made according to these forms. They shall also prepare and distribute the proper forms, to be signed by the school commissioners of each district respectively, certifying under their hands that they have adopted and used in their respective districts the text books directed to be used by the State Board of Education, and no other, except in branches in which said Board has given no direction; and the Auditor of Accounts shall neither settle with, nor give any order, or certificate, to any school district, its clerk, or commissioners, until such certificate shall be presented and filed with him. *[margin notes: Annual meeting. Who shall be Secretary. Who President. Powers and duties of Board. Shall determine what text books are to be used. Who shall issue blanks. Returns. Shall prepare and distribute forms. When the Auditor shall not settle.]*

The members of the State Board of Education shall receive no salary or compensation for the performance of the duties thereof. A majority of the members of the State Board of Education shall constitute a quorum to do business, but a less number may adjourn from time to time, until a quorum be obtained. Their Secretary shall keep a record of their proceedings, and all books, papers, and other documents, shall be carefully preserved by the Secretary and be by him handed over to his successor in office. *[margin notes: Sec. 3, Chap. 46, Vol. 16. No compensation. Quorum. Duties of Secretary.]*

The provisions of this article, and of the two preceding articles, shall not apply to any school or school districts managed or controlled by an incorporated board of education, unless by special request of said board. *[margin notes: Sec. 10, Chap. 46, Vol. 16. Not applicable to incorporated schools. Exception.]*

ARTICLE IV.

DISTRICTS.

R. C. Chap. 42, Sec. 1.

Limits of districts to be recorded.

The limits of the school districts in the several counties, and all alterations of such limits, whether by the division of a district, the union of several, or otherwise, shall be recorded in the office of the Clerk of the Peace of the proper county.

Certificate of Clerk of Peace to Trustee of School Fund.

The Clerk of the Peace shall certify, in due form, to the Trustee of the School Fund, the number and location of each school district laid out by the Levy Court of his county, and every alteration of a district.

Alteration of districts.

Notice to alter district.

The Levy Court, two-thirds of all the members concurring, may, upon application, make such alterations, having due regard to the public convenience, and to the interest of the schools; but notice of such intended application, and of the time when it will be made, and of the alterations desired, shall be given by advertisements posted in four or more public places in each district to be affected by the change twenty days before the application is made, or the court shall not receive it.

Chap. 442, Sec. 2, Vol. 11.

Application to divide district.

Appointment of commissioners.

Mode of proceeding in dividing district.

Return of commissioners.

Whenever a petition shall be presented to the Levy Court of either county, signed by twelve or more owners or holders of real estate in any school district or districts contiguous to each other, praying that an additional district may be formed from the district or districts in which they reside, the said Levy Court shall appoint three judicious and impartial persons, residing in said county, and without the limits of the districts immediately affected by the petition, who shall go to the said district or districts, and inquire concerning the propriety of laying out an additional district therefrom; and if, after careful examination, the said commissioners should be of opinion that an additional district should be laid off, they shall locate and lay off such additional district as to them shall seem just and proper; and when the said commissioners, or a majority of them, shall have located and laid out said additional district, they, or a majority of them, shall make return of the said additional district so located and laid out, and also of the part or parts of the original district or districts remaining after the said additional district shall have been laid off, describing plainly the metes and bounds of each, into the office of the Clerk of the Peace of said county, to be by him filed among the records of his said office, and within ten days thereafter the said Clerk of the Peace shall make a copy thereof and deliver the same to the Trustee of the School Fund. From and after the time of such return by the commissioners into the office of the Clerk of the Peace, the additional district so located and laid off shall be deemed and taken to be a school district of said county, and numbered in continuation of school districts in said county, and all the acts of the General Assembly of this State, for the general regulation, government, and benefit of free schools, shall be extended and applied to said additional district; and the Trustee of the School Fund, in the distribution of the school fund applicable to school districts in said county, shall give to said additional district an equal proportion of the money in his hands applicable to school districts in said county. No such additional district shall be located and laid off by the commissioners† unless it shall be made satisfactorily to appear that there will be left remaining in the original school district, or if more than one, [in each of] the original districts out of which it is proposed to be laid out, at least thirty-five scholars over the age of five years, and also a like number in the said additional school district proposed to be laid out. †In case said commissioners shall determine that no additional district is necessary, they shall make return thereof to the Clerk of the Peace of said county, to be filed in his office.

Provisions of Free School Law applicable to additional district.

†Chap. 296, Sec. 1, Vol. 12.
See Rev. Code, page 214, &c.
Must be 35 scholars left in original district.

†Chap. 442, Sec. 2, Vol. 11.
See Rev. Code, page 213.

It shall be the duty of the persons appointed by the Levy Court to lay off districts as aforesaid, or a majority of them, to give notice, in writing, at least ten days before the holding of the first regular meeting of the school voters to be held in districts created as aforesaid, of the time and place for holding such meeting, which notice shall be posted in five of the most public places in the district. A failure to give notice as aforesaid shall in no wise affect or invalidate an organization that may be made by the school voters in such districts, *provided* that a majority of the school voters of the district be present at any meeting held without notice given as aforesaid.

Chap. 139, Sec. 1, Vol. 13.
See Rev. Code, page 216.
Notice of first regular meetings in new districts.

Proviso.

The commissioners, before entering upon the duties prescribed, shall each take an oath, or affirmation, to perform the same with fidelity. They shall each receive one dollar for each days' service, to be allowed by the Levy Court of said county.

Chap. 442, Sec. 3, Vol. 11.
Commissioners to be sworn.
Their compensation—how paid.

2

Chap. 442, Sec. 4, Vol. 11.
See Rev. Code, page 213.
Inhabitants of add'l district to enjoy benefits of school in original district till next stated meeting.

In case any additional district is created under the provisions of this act, in order that none may be even temporarily deprived of a school, the inhabitants of the portion of the district or districts included within said additional district shall continue to have and enjoy, as before, the privileges and benefit of the school in the original district or districts from which they were taken until the day of the next annual stated meeting of the school voters in this State, when they can organize.

Chap. 442, Sec. 5, Vol. 11.
See Rev. Code, page 213.
Site, how procured.

In case the school commissioners of any school district shall not be able to procure, by agreement with the owner, a lot of land suitable and proper for the erection of a school house for the use of the district, it shall and may be lawful for the said school commissioners to apply to the Levy Court of their county. who shall thereupon appoint three judicious and impartial freeholders of said county, residing without the limits of said school district, to select a site for such school house and appurtenances, not to exceed half an acre in any case. The said commissioners shall, as soon as conveniently possible after the said appointment, notify the said freeholders and fix a day when they shall meet in said district to select such site, and shall also give notice to the inhabitants of said district of the time so fixed, by notices posted in five of the most public places in said district at least ten days before the day of meeting. The said freeholders shall, on the day so fixed, proceed to the said district, taking with them a surveyor, if necessary, and shall select such site as they may deem most suitable for the purposes aforesaid, and shall cause a plot and description of the same to be made out and delivered to the commissioners, who shall, within thirty days after such delivery, lodge the same in the Recorder's office of the proper county, to be recorded.

Chap. 442, Sec. 6, Vol. 11.
See Rev. Code, page 213, &c.
Assessment of damages.

The said freeholders shall also, at the time of selecting and locating the site, assess the damages of the owner or owners, taking into consideration all circumstances of convenience or injury, but in making such assessment they shall allow at least the cash value of the land taken, and shall certify their award to both parties, owners and commissioners, whereupon, upon payment of the damages so assessed, the said land so taken shall become and be the property of the said school district for the purpose aforesaid. In case any such owner or owners

Case of minor or non-resident.

be a minor, non-resident, or from any cause incapable of receiving, or unwilling or neglecting to receive said damages, the said school commissioners may deposit the same, to the credit of such owner or owners, in the Farmers' Bank of the State of Delaware, or any branch thereof, and such deposit shall operate as payment.

In case the said freeholders should fail to meet on the day fixed, the commissioners may call them out again upon like notice to the district, as above provided. The said freeholders shall have power to adjourn from time to time. The decision of a majority shall be as good as that of the whole. The fees of the freeholders shall be one dollar per day. All the expenses shall be borne by the district. *Chap. 442. Sec. 7, Vol. 11. See Rev. Code, page 214. Further provisions in regard to freeholders.*

Each school district, by name of "School District No. —, in —— County," or "United School District, Nos. —, in —— County," (as the case may be, and filling the blanks properly,) may take and hold ground for a school house, and the appurtenances and furniture; may take and hold by devise, bequest, or donation, real and personal estate, not exceeding in clear annual income one thousand dollars, for the use of the free school in said district, and may alien the same; may take bond from the collector; may prosecute actions upon it, and any action for injury done to any property of the district, in which action they shall recover double damages and costs; and also any action for a forfeiture or penalty due to the district. Any of the said actions may be brought before a Justice of the Peace, if the sum demanded do not exceed one hundred dollars, and he shall proceed as in other demands of like amount. A school district shall not possess any other corporate power or franchise. *R. C. Chap. 42, Sec. 22. Capacity of school district, its powers.*

The following districts have been sub-divided and new districts formed therefrom :

IN NEW CASTLE COUNTY.

District No. 54, new District No.

Districts Nos. 2, 3, new District No. 73.

Districts Nos. 57, 58, 59, new District No 74.

Districts Nos. 8, 19, 23, new District No. 75.

District No. 21.

District No. 62.

Districts Nos. 21, 33 and 38. Chapter 34, Volume 11, passed February 9th, 1853.

District No. 19. Chapter 272, Volume 11, passed March 1st, 1855.

Districts Nos. 69, 71 and 72. Chapter 293, Volume 11, passed March 2d, 1855.

Districts Nos. 61 and 65.   Chapter 295, Volume 11, passed March 2d, 1855.

District No. 62.   Chapter 338, Volume 11, passed February 4th, 1857.

Districts Nos. 65, 72 and 80.   Chapter 345, Volume 11, passed February 10th, 1857.

District No. 34, Chapter 411, Volume 11, passed February 27th, 1857.

Districts Nos. 56 and 57.   Chapter 456, Volume 11, passed March 4th, 1857.

Districts Nos. 59, 60 and 61.   Chapter 464, Volume 11, passed March 4th, 1857.

Districts Nos. 3 and 8.   Chapter 532, Volume 11, passed February 2d, 1859.

District No. 60.   Chapter 594, Volume 11, passed February 18th, 1859.   .

District No. 20.   Chapter 424, Volume 13, passed February 18th, 1869.

Districts Nos. 71, 72 and 80.   Chapter 30, Volume 16, passed February 19th, 1879.

An act to transfer certain real estate from one school district to another in New Castle county.   Chapter 399, Volume 14, passed March 20th, 1873.

Certain real estate of Lorenzo D. Ginn transferred from School District No. 81 to School District No. 72.   Chapter 37, Volume 15, passed March 2d, 1875.

Boundary of School District No. 81 changed.   Chapter 41, Volume 15, passed February 23d, 1875.

District No. 21 divided.   Chapter 33, Volume 16, passed March 10th, 1879.

Certain real estate of Joab S. Alston transferred from District No. 88 to District No. 53.   Chapter 43, Volume 16, passed March 27th, 1879.

Boundary line of School District No. 54 changed.   Chapter 356, Volume 16, passed February 25th, 1881.

Certain real estate of George W. Sparks, Preston Lea and John C. Corbit transferred from District No. 61 to District No. 79.   Chapter 357, Volume 16, passed March 1st, 1881.

All of District No. 20½ not included in the 11th Ward of the city of Wilmington shall be a portion of School District No. 20.   Chapter 374, Volume 16, passed April 9th, 1881.

Certain property in District No. 48 removed.   Chapter 49, Volume 15, passed March 25th, 1875.

IN KENT COUNTY.

Districts Nos. 15, 16, 19, 20, new District No. 46.

Districts Nos. 2, 4, 9, 10, new District No. 49.

District No. 27, new District No. 50.

Districts Nos. 10, 11, 13, 17, new District No. 51.

Districts Nos. 29, 30, 33, 34, new District No. 52.

Districts Nos. 24, 25, new District No. 53—returned as 52.

District No. 45.   Chapter 11, Volume 11, passed February 24th, 1853.

District No. 31.   Chapter 368, Volume 11, passed March 1st, 1855.

Districts Nos. 33, 35 and 36.   Chapter 274, Volume 11, passed March 1st, 1855.

District No. 25.   Chapter 374, Volume 11, passed February 19th, 1857.

Districts Nos. 40 and 41.   Chapter 384, Volume 11, passed February 23d, 1857.

Districts Nos. 24, 29 and 30.   Chapter 427, Volume 11, passed March 2d, 1857.

Districts Nos. 38, 35 and 30.   Chapter 457, Volume 11, passed March 4th, 1857.

Districts Nos. 37 and 39.   Chapter 460, Volume 11, passed March 4th, 1857.

Districts Nos. 3 and 5, Chapter 565, Volume 11, passed February 14th, 1859.

Districts Nos. 74, 37 and 34. Chapter 50, Volume 14, passed March 6th, 1871.

All that district lying between "Old Duck Creek" and the "Delaware Bay," known as "Bombay Hook Island," has been created an additional school district by Chapter 423, Volume 13, passed February 17th, 1869.

Certain real estate of Alfred Hudson and John Anthony transferred from District No. 84 to District No. 2. Chapter 53, Volume 14, passed March 29th, 1871.

Certain real estate of Cyrus P. Rodgers transferred from School District No. 110 to United School District Nos. 32, 75, 76 and 78. Chapter 38, Volume 15, passed March 16th, 1875.

Certain real estate of Richbell Allaband transferred from School District No. 21 to United School District Nos. 113 and 113½. Chapter 364, Volume 15, passed February 27th, 1877.

District No. 27 divided. Chapter 368, Volume 15, passed March 19th, 1877.

District No. 121 dissolved and certain real estate of William H. Dickerson transferred to No. 94. Chapter 39, Volume 16, passed March 19th, 1879.

School District No. 39 divided. Chapter 372, Volume 16, passed April 8th, 1881.

IN SUSSEX COUNTY.

District No. 25, new District No. 25½.

District No. 53, new District No. —.

District No. 65, new District No. 65½.

District No. 73, new District No. 73½.

District No. 27, new District No. —.

District No. 49, new District No. 49½.

Districts Nos. 3, 4, 5, 6, new District No. 79.

Districts Nos. 36, 40, 41, 43, new District No. 79, really 80.

District No. 77, new District No. 77½.

District No. 24, new District No. 24½.

Districts Nos. 41, 42, 44, new District No. 42½.

Districts Nos. 43, 44, new District No. —.

Districts Nos. 19, 20, 21, 22, new District No. 82.

Districts Nos. 13, 33, 52, 63, new District No. 81.

Districts Nos. 42, 53 and 54. Chapter 10, Volume 11, passed January 24th, 1853.

Districts Nos. 50 and 51. Chapter 48, Volume 11, passed February 21st, 1853.

Districts Nos. 74 and 75. Chapter 83, Volume 11, passed February 24th, 1853.

Districts Nos. 54, 62 and 63. Chapter 177, Volume 11, passed February 2d, 1855.

Districts Nos. 78 and 3. Chapter 267, Volume 11, passed March 1st, 1855.

Districts Nos. 48 and 39. Chapter 282, Volume 11, passed March 2d, 1855.

Districts Nos. 16, 18 and 19. Chapter 328, Volume 11, passed January 29th, 1857.

District No. 75. Chapter 363, Volume 11, passed February 17th, 1857.

District No. 38. Chapter 375, Volume 11, passed February 19th, 1857.

Districts Nos. 81, 13 and 11. Chapter 382, Volume 11, passed February 20th, 1857.

District No. 59. Chapter 387, Volume 11, passed February 23d, 1857.

Districts Nos. 78, 66, 77 and 77½. Chapter 402, Volume 11, passed February 26th, 1857.

Section of country between Districts Nos. 30, 31 and 32 made District No. 87. Chapter 420, Volume 11, passed February 28th, 1857.

Districts Nos. 102, 69, 109 and 161.   Chapter 425, Volume 13, passed March 18th, 1869, and revived by Chapter 52, Volume 14.

William Adams, Henry Adams and George Adams changed from District No. 168 to District No. 50, by Chapter 181, Volume 14, passed March 23d, 1871.

District No. 57.   Chapter 398, Volume 14, passed March 13th, 1873.

Certain real estate of Isaac G. Phillips transferred from School District No. 168 to School District No. 50.   Chapter 36, Volume 15, passed January 27th, 1875.

Certain real estate of John A. Nicholson, G. W. S. Nicholson, Henry Q. Nicholson and L. W. Muse transferred from School District No. 76 to School District No. 72.   Chapter 39, Volume 15, passed March 17th, 1875.

United School District Nos. 46 and 133 enlarged by taking certain real estate from District No. 60.   Chapter 40, Volume 15, passed February 10th, 1875.

Districts Nos. 109, 68 and 158.   Chapter 360, Volume 15, passed February 1st, 1877.

Certain real estate of George W. Horsey transferred from School District No. 46 to No. 51.   Chapter 363, Volume 15, passed February 26th, 1877.

Certain real estate of Robert Lambden transferred from School Districts Nos. 45 and 83 to United School Districts Nos. 44 and 150.   Chapter 29, Volume 16, passed February 3th, 1879.

Certain real estate of Mrs. A. G. Woodruff transferred from School District No. 75 to District No. 91.   Chapter 31, Volume 16, passed March 5th, 1879.

Certain real estate of R. E. Deimer transferred from School District No. 75 to No. 91.   Chapter 34, Volume 16, passed March 11th, 1879.

Districts Nos. 56 and 162 consolidated and numbered 56, with power to draw only one dividend.   Chapter 35, Volume 16, passed March 12th, 1879.

Certain real estate of Daniel Short transferred from District No. 94 to District No. 122.   Chapter 41, Volume 16, March 21st, 1879.

Certain real estate of Samuel Kinney and Samuel Kinney, Jr., transferred from School District No. 48 to No. 148.   Chapter 42, Volume 16, passed March 25th, 1879.

Certain real estate of William C. Hern and Edward R. Hern transferred from School District No. 126 to No. 38.   Chapter 44, Volume 16, passed March 28th, 1879.

Certain real estate of Cyrus Q. Fooks, Daniel Short and others, transferred from School District No. 42 to No. 122.   Chapter 363, Volume 16, passed March 24th, 1881.

ARTICLE V.

UNION OF SCHOOL DISTRICTS.

R. C. Chap. 42, Sec. 8.   Two or more school districts, in any county, may unite for establishing and supporting a free school for their common benefit ; and such districts, when united, shall be one district by the name of

Name of united district.   " United School District Nos. ——, in —— County."

The manner of forming a union of districts shall be this :

1. Notice shall be given in each district which it is proposed to unite, as required for stated meetings in the several districts.

Notice to unite.

2. At the meeting, thus called in each district, if two-thirds of the voters present are in favor of the union, a committee of three of such voters shall be appointed to arrange the terms, and the meeting may be adjourned to hear their report ; if a majority of them agree upon a union with any other district, or districts, and settle the terms thereof, the same shall be reported to an adjourned meeting, and if such report shall be adopted by two-thirds of the voters present, it shall be obligatory, and the districts mentioned shall be united : *provided* like proceedings be had in all the said districts ; but if, in either district, the report be not adopted by a vote of two-thirds, this shall not defeat the union between the other districts so adopting it ; they shall be united and the other shall be excluded.

Votes necessary to a union.

Appointment of committee to arrange terms of union.

Report of committee.

Proviso.

3. A meeting of the united district shall then be held at the time and place fixed by the terms of the union. At this meeting a school committee for the united school district shall be chosen, and a vote may be passed to raise money by contribution, but not by tax. This meeting shall also inquire into the proceedings preparatory to the union of the districts ; and its determination thereupon shall be conclusive.

First meeting of united districts.

Business of.

United school districts shall have the same powers and exercise them in the same manner as original districts. The power of taxation shall extend to the amount that could lawfully be raised by tax in the several districts composing such united district if acting separately. [But United School Districts Nos. 23 and 75, in New Castle County, may, so long as they remain united, raise, by taxation, one thousand dollars annually ; and if they disunite and become separate districts, each of the said districts may raise, by taxation, five hundred dollars annually.] The union of districts shall not affect the account of the Trustee of the School Fund ; but dividends of the income of the fund shall be apportioned and credited to the original districts, as before the union ; and all sums placed to the credit of the several districts, of which the union is formed, shall be paid upon the order of the school committee of the united district, and applied to the use of such district, upon their showing that a sum has been raised sufficient to entitle these several districts to draw their dividends.

R. C. Chap. 42, Sec. 9.

Powers of united district to tax.

Districts Nos. 23 and 75, N. C. Co. may levy tax of $1000 annually.

United district entitled to dividends of the several districts of which it is composed.

Place of meeting of the school voters.   The place of meeting of school voters of an united district shall be the school house of the district; or, if there be none, then one at the school house mentioned in the notices, which shall conform to any standing order of the school voters.

Proposal to have several school houses in a united district.   A proposal to have several school houses in an united district may be brought before a regular meeting of the school voters by inserting it in the notices of such meeting. If such proposal is made, the Secretary shall inquire concerning the regularity of the notice, and make a minute of the facts. If it be carried, the school committee shall have power to execute it.

R. C. Chap. 42, Sec. 10.
Joint primary schools.
† Chap. 40, Vol. 16.   The respective school committees of adjoining districts shall have power to make such arrangements, in establishing a school for small children over six† years old, for the joint benefit of such adjoining districts, as they may deem proper.

[For consolidation, or re-districting, by Superintendent, see Article 1, page 5.]

The following are the districts which have been consolidated, with corporate powers, by acts of Assembly:

School Districts Nos. 8, 12, 93 and 160, in Sussex county, incorporated under the name of the " Milton Academy." Chapter 484, Volume 13, passed April 7th, 1869; amended by Chapter 370, Volume 15, passed February 7th, 1877.

School Districts Nos. 70, 102, 70½ and 102, in Sussex county, incorporated under the name of the " Seaford Public Schools." Chapter 45, Volume 15, passed March 17th, 1875; amended by Chapter 362, Volume 15, passed February 16th, 1877.

School Districts Nos. 52 and 76, in New Castle county, incorporated under the name of the " Delaware City Public Schools." Chapter 52, Volume 15, passed March 4th, 1875.

School Districts Nos. 14, 15, 110 and 112, in Sussex county, incorporated under the name of the " Board of Public Education for the Town of Lewes." Chapter 53, Volume 15, passed March 19th, 1875; amended by Chapter 372, Volume 15, passed March 23d, 1877.

School Districts embraced in the limits of the city of New Castle, New Castle county, incorporated under the name of the " Board of Public Education for the City of New Castle." Chapter 54, Volume 15, passed March 10th, 1875.

School Districts Nos. 60 and 94, in New Castle county, incorporated under the name of the " Middletown Schools." Chapter 357, Volume 15, passed January 29th, 1877; amended by Chapter 359, same volume.

School Districts Nos. 6 and 95, in Kent county, consolidated and called District No. 6. Chapter 361, Volume 15, passed February 9th, 1877.

School Districts Nos. 65 and 66 and United School Districts Nos. 42, 43, 68 and 70, in Kent county, consolidated under the name of "The Public Schools of Milford, Kent county." Chapter 365, Volume 15, passed March 8th, 1877.

School Districts Nos. 50 and 108, in Kent county, consolidated under the name of "The Magnolia Public Schools." Chapter 367, Volume 15, passed March 12th, 1877.

School Districts Nos. 18, 60, 90, 91, 92 and 101, in Kent county, incorporated under the name of "The Board of Education of the Dover Public Schools." Chapter 371, Volume 15, passed February 26th, 1877.

School Districts Nos. 56 and 162, in Sussex county, consolidated into one school district and called No. 56. Chapter 35, Volume 16, passed March 12th, 1879.

School Districts Nos. 27 and 122, in Kent county, consolidated into one school district under the name of the "Lebanon Public Schools." Chapter 38, Volume 16, passed March 9th, 1879.

School Districts Nos. 32 and 108, in Sussex county, consolidated under the name of "The Selbyville Public Schools." Chapter 358, Volume 16, passed March 8th, 1881; supplemented by Chapter 367, Volume 16, passed March 31st, 1881.

School Districts Nos. 152 and 80, in Sussex county, consolidated under the name of "The Lowe's X Roads Public Schools." Chapter 360, Volume 16, passed March 16th, 1881; supplemented by Chapter 368, Volume 16, passed March 31st, 1881.

School Districts Nos. 26 and 112, in Kent county, united into one school district under the title of "The Canterbury Public Schools." Chapter 364, Volume 16, passed March 25th, 1881.

School Districts Nos. 67, 96, 106 and 107, in Sussex county, united under the name of "The Board of Commissioners of the Public Schools of Georgetown, Sussex County." Chapter 365, Volume 16, passed March 29th, 1881.

United School District Nos. 3 and 77, and United School District Nos. 5 and 107, in Kent county, united under the name of the "Smyrna Public Schools." Chapter 366, Volume 16, passed March 30th, 1881.

The Wilmington Districts, consisting of Nos. 3, 9, 10, 11, 12, 13, 14, 15, 16, 17, 18 and 19, in New Castle county, were consolidated by the following acts, viz: "An act for the benefit of public schools in Wilmington," passed at Dover, February 9th, 1852; "An act to amend the act for the benefit of public schools in Wilmington," passed at Dover, January 20th, 1853; "A supplement to the act for the benefit of public schools in Wilmington," passed at Dover, February 10th, 1855; "An act to amend the act for the benefit of public schools in Wilmington," passed at Dover, March 3d, 1857; "A further supplement to the act for the benefit of public schools in Wilmington," passed at Dover, February 25th, 1859; "An act in addition to the act for the benefit of public schools in Wilmington," passed at Dover, February 11th, 1863; "An act in further addition to the act for the benefit of public schools in Wilmington," passed at Dover, January 22d, 1869; "An act to amend the further supplement, passed at Dover, February 24th, 1869, to the act entitled 'An act to amend Chapter 73 of the Revised Statutes,'" passed at Dover, March 30th, 1869; "An additional supplement to the act entitled 'An act for the benefit of public schools in Wilmington,'" passed at Dover, February 24th, 1871; "A further supplement to the act for the benefit of public schools in Wilmington," passed at Dover, February 24th, 1871; "A further supplement to the act for the benefit of public schools in Wilmington," passed at Dover, April

8th, 1873; "An act to annex, for school purposes, School District No. 19, in New Castle county, to the city of Wilmington," passed at Dover, March 10th, 1875; "An act to amend an act entitled 'An additional supplement to the act entitled 'An act for the benefit of public schools in Wilmington,' '" passed at Dover, March 22d, 1877; "A further supplement to an act entitled 'An act to amend an act entitled 'An additional supplement to the act entitled 'An act for the benefit of public schools in Wilmington,' '" passed at Dover, March 6th, 1879; "An act to further amend the charter of the city of Wilmington, Section 13 thereof," passed at Dover, April 1st, 1869; "An act in relation to taxation in certain parts of the city of Wilmington," passed at Dover, March 15th, 1877; "A further supplement to the act entitled 'An act to limit the city debt of Wilmington and to provide for the discharge thereof,'" passed at Dover, March 20th, 1877; "A further supplement to an act entitled 'An act to amend an act entitled 'An additional supplement to the act entitled 'An act for the benefit of the public schools of Wilmington,' '" passed at Dover, March 6th, 1879; "A further supplement to the act for the benefit of public schools in Wilmington," passed at Dover, April 8th, 1881.

ARTICLE VI.

STATED MEETINGS.

R. C. Chap. 42, Sec. 3.
Stated annual meetings.

The school voters in each district shall hold a stated meeting every year, on the first Saturday of April, at two o'clock in the afternoon, at the place appointed by the Levy Court, until there shall be a school house for the district, and then at such school house; the meeting shall

Meeting kept open one hour.
Exception.
Chap. 36, Vol. 16.

be kept open at least one hour. [Except School District No. 8, in New Castle county—the hour for holding the annual meeting therein is from 4½ o'clock to 6 o'clock, P. M.]

Qualification of school voter.
† Vol. 12, Chap. 391, Sec. 1.

Every person residing within the district and having right to vote for Representatives in the General Assembly,† and having paid his school tax for the preceding year, shall be a school voter of said district.

Penalty for illegal voting.

And if any person, not being so qualified, shall vote at any meeting of school voters therein, he shall be deemed guilty of a misdemeanor, and shall be fined fifteen dollars.

Quorum of voters.

Any number of voters present may proceed to business, and their acts shall be valid.

Chairman and secretary elected
† Chap. 138, Sec. 2, Vol. 13.
One member of committee elected by ballot for 3 years.

They shall appoint a chairman and secretary, and then elect by ballot, by a majority of votes from the school voters,† at every annual meeting, one member of the school committee to serve for the term of three years as a successor to the member whose term shall at that time expire, [according to Chapter 138, Volume 13,] and shall likewise elect to fill all vacancies or unexpired terms occasioned by death, or otherwise, of any member of said committees. *Vacancies to be filled at stated meetings.*

The school voters shall then resolve, by a majority of votes, what sum shall be raised in said district for a school house or a free school therein. They shall then proceed to vote by ballot respecting a tax; and if a majority of the votes be "*for a tax,*" the sum so resolved to be raised may be levied by taxation. If the majority of the votes be "*against a tax,*" the sum so resolved to be raised may be raised by subscription. *R. C. Chap. 42, Sec. 3. Resolution to raise money. Vote by ballot for tax. Sum resolved may be raised by subscription.*

When a majority of the voters of any school district, at their annual meeting in April, wish to raise by tax more than the amount provided for in Article XI, for the support of a free school in their district, they shall resolve, by a majority of votes, what sum shall be raised for that purpose : *provided* said sum does not exceed the sum of four hundred dollars, exclusive of the amount provided by Article XI. *Chap. 70, Sec. 2, Vol. 12. Larger sum for school may be raised by tax— not to exceed $400.*

When a majority of the voters of any school district, at their annual meeting in April, wish to raise by tax any sum of money not exceeding five hundred dollars, for the purpose of building or repairing a school house in their district, they shall resolve by a majority of votes what sum shall be raised in said district for that purpose. *Chap. 70, Sec. 3, Vol. 12. Money for school house may be raised by tax— not to exceed $500.*

No vote respecting a tax shall be taken at any other time than the stated annual meeting, or the substitute therefor. Any district, upon raising the sum of three hundred dollars in any year, by tax, may, in addition thereto, levy such further sum as may be required for a good school therein, by quarterly apportionment, in the discretion of the committee, on the persons sending scholars to such school, unless a majority of the voters, at the stated annual meeting, direct otherwise. The sums so apportioned may be collected in the same manner that the school taxes are collected, and the collector and his sureties shall be liable, on his bond, for the same, as for taxes. *R. C. Chap. 42, Sec. 3. Any district raising $300 may raise, by quarterly apportionment, on persons sending scholars, such sum as may be required for a good school.*

A stated meeting, after appointing a chairman and secretary, may adjourn; and the proceedings of the adjourned meeting shall be of the same nature and force, except as to a tax, as if had at the original meeting. *When a stated meeting may adjourn.*

If the annual stated meeting shall not be held in any district, or if

R. C. Chap. 42,
Sec. 7.

Failure to hold
annual meeting.

Other meetings
may be held.

the school committee shall not then be appointed, or a resolution to raise money passed, the district shall not thereby lose the power to proceed, but meetings, adjourned, occasional, or stated, may be held; and if there be no clerk, or commissioner, of the district to give notice of a stated meeting, it shall be given by the Clerk of the Peace, on application of five or more of the school voters of such district, by advertisements, posted as required for other stated meetings.

R. C. Chap. 42,
Sec. 11.

The school committee of each district, elected as aforesaid, shall continue in office until successors to them are duly elected.

Vacancies in
committee, how
filled.
To be sworn or
affirmed.

Vacancies in the committee may be filled at any adjourned or occasional meeting. Each of the committee shall be sworn or affirmed to perform his duty with fidelity.

ARTICLE VII.

OCCASIONAL MEETINGS.

R. C. Chap. 42,
Sec. 5.

Occasional meet-
ings, how called.

Place.

Occasional meetings of the school voters of a district may be called by the school committee, by advertisement stating the business of the meeting, and posted as required for stated meetings. They must be held at the place where the stated meetings are held.

Quorum present
necessary to act.

Any number of the school voters, met pursuant to such call, may appoint a chairman and secretary, and transact any business mentioned

Duty of secre-
tary.

in the advertisements, but no other. The secretary shall make a note of the business mentioned in the advertisements, and where and when they were posted. These entries shall be conclusive, unless proved

Penalty for
fraudulent entry.

fraudulent; and the making a fraudulent entry shall be a misdemeanor, punishable by fine not exceeding one hundred dollars.

ARTICLE VIII.

RETURNS.

R. C. Chap. 42,
Sec. 6.

Return of pro-
ceedings of
school voters.

Two certificates of the proceedings of every meeting of school voters shall be made and signed by the chairman and secretary; one shall be delivered to the clerk of the district, the other to the Clerk of

When made, by
whom.

the Peace of the county, to be kept as a public record. If the chairman, or secretary, shall neglect his duty in this respect, for the space

Penalty for neg-
lect, $50.

of one month, he shall be deemed guilty of a misdemeanor, and be fined fifty dollars.

If the certificates be not so delivered within one month, the proceedings of the meeting shall be void; and the school committee in *Proceedings void.* office, next before such meeting, shall continue in office, so far as to *Who may call another meeting.* call another meeting, and shall proceed to do so, by advertisements, posted as required for stated meetings. A statement that the proceedings of the last meeting have not been duly returned, shall be a sufficient statement of the business; and at a meeting so called, the school voters shall have power to do any act which they could do at *Power of such meeting.* the preceding meeting; and the meeting shall be regulated by the law applicable to the preceding meeting, and shall be a substitute therefor.

ARTICLE IX.

GENERAL POWERS AND DUTIES OF COMMISSIONERS AND CLERKS.

The powers and duties of school committees shall be: *R. C. Chap. 42, Sec. 11.*

1. To determine the site; lease or purchase the necessary ground, *Duties and powers of committee.* and build or procure a suitable house for the district. The school *Location of school house.* house shall be as near the centre of the district as practicable; when it is built, or procured, it shall not be removed, nor another procured, *School house, when moved.* without the direction of the school voters at a stated meeting.

2. To keep the school house in good repair, and supply it with *To be kept in good repair.* necessary furniture and fuel; to bring actions, if necessary, for any injury to it.

3. To provide a school for the district, when, and as long as their *R. C. Chap. 42, Sec. 11.* funds will enable them; and to employ teachers. They shall employ *Employment of teachers.* no teacher whom they shall not have just ground to believe to be of *Qualifications of teachers.* good moral character, and well qualified to teach reading, writing, arithmetic, and English grammar, and such other branches of knowl- *Sec. 9, Chap. 46, Vol. 16.* edge as they may deem necessary to be taught in their district, and *Persons not holding certificates shall not be employed.* who does not hold a certificate from the State Superintendent. And any one so employed shall receive no compensation whatever; but the Superintendent may issue temporary permits to teach for a period *Temporary permits.* not exceeding thirty days, when, in his judgment, the interests of education require it. They may employ a female teacher when and *Female teachers.* for such parts of the year as they may deem best to do so. They may dismiss a teacher. They may make regulations for the government of *Committee may make rules for government of school.* the school, and by these may provide for the expulsion of a scholar for obstinate misbehavior. The school shall be free to all the white children of the district, over six years old.

Funds of district.   4. To receive and collect all money belonging to, appropriated, or resolved to be raised for the district, and to apply the same justly.

To appoint collectors.   5. To appoint collectors for the district, and take security, by bond, which may be in this form :

Bond, form of.   " KNOW ALL MEN BY THESE PRESENTS, *That we, —— ——, are firmly bound, jointly and severally, to School District No. ——, in —— county, in the sum of ——, to be paid to said school district ; sealed with our seals and dated the —— day of ——, 18——. The condition of the above written obligation is such, that if the said ————, who is collector of the school district aforesaid, shall well and faithfully execute said office and perform all his duties as such collector, then the said obligation shall be void.*"

6. To do all acts requisite for effecting the premises.

Quorum of committee may act.   The acts of a majority of the school committees shall be as effectual, in all cases, as if done by them all.

R. C. Chap. 42, Sec. 19.
Committee to post two copies of the account.
Penalty.   It shall be the duty of the school committee to post two copies of the account settled, as required by Article XV, in public places of the district, within ten days after the settlement ; and if they neglect this duty, they shall forfeit and pay to the district ten dollars.

R. C. Chap. 42, Sec. 20.
Committee report to stated meeting.   The school committee shall, annually, at the stated meeting, exhibit a just account of their receipts and expenditures and a report of all their proceedings. The meeting may appoint persons to settle said account.

Committee to pay over money to successors.   The said committee shall pay to their successors in office all money due from them, and if they neglect to do so for ten days, they shall forfeit and pay, additionally, the rate of twenty-five per cent. on the sum due.

Allowance of committee.   The committee shall receive no emolument ; but for attendance before the Auditor, they shall be allowed, in their account, each one dollar per day, and three cents per mile of necessary travel.

R. C. Chap. 42, Sec. 4.
Notice of stated meetings.   It shall be the duty of the clerk of the district to give notice of the stated meetings, by advertisements, under hand, of the day, hour and place thereof, posted in five or more public places of the district, at **Penalty for neglect $10.** least five days before the meeting ; and if he neglects this duty, he shall forfeit and pay to the district ten dollars ; but the want of such **Commissioners to give notice when no clerk.** notice shall not make the acts of the meeting void. If there be no clerk, the commissioners shall give the notice under the same penalty.

The clerk of the district shall keep a record book of the district, in R. C. Chap. 42, Sec. 21.
which he shall enter its bounds and description and any changes Record book of district—what
therein, a copy of the certificate of the proceedings of every meeting to contain.
of the school voters, the proceedings of the school committee, and the
names of the scholars attending the school, a list of whom shall be
furnished by the teachers. This book shall be evidence. He shall
also keep all papers belonging to the district, or to the committee.

It shall be the duty of the clerk of each school district to distrib- Sec. 6, Chap. 369, Vol. 16.
ute the books received from the State Superintendent, as aforesaid, Distribution of school books
to the scholars of the district, or their parents, guardian, or other by clerks.
person, as they may desire, upon the receipt of the price for the same, How paid for.
which shall be forwarded by him to the State Superintendent within
thirty days thereafter. The clerk of each district shall be responsible
for the safe keeping of the books furnished him by the Superintendent Safe keeping of books.
as aforesaid, and also for the price of the books sold to parents, guar-
dians, scholars, or other persons. Any money, or the value of the Remedy for default in clerks.
books which such clerk may fail to account for, according to law, may
be recovered in the name of the State by the State Superintendent,
before a Justice of the Peace, as other accounts, when the amount
does not exceed the sum of one hundred dollars. Such clerk shall Report of clerk.
also make a report to the State Treasurer quarterly of the number of
books, and their kind and price, supplied by the State Superintendent
as aforesaid, and at the expiration of his term of office shall turn over
to his successor in office all the books on hand and take a receipt for
the same, which shall be his voucher in settlement.

ARTICLE X.

TEACHERS.

It shall be the duty of every teacher employed under the provisions Sec. 12, Chap. 46, Vol. 16.
of this act to make out and hand to the commissioners of the district, Quarterly reports.
at the end of each quarter, a report, setting forth the whole number What to contain.
of pupils attending school during the quarter, designating whether
male or female, the number of days each has attended, the books used
and branches taught; and until such report shall have been made, it When teacher's salary shall be
shall not be lawful for the commissioners to pay such teacher his or her withheld.
salary. The reports made in pursuance of the previous provision shall

When reports shall be forwarded to the Superintendent.

be forwarded annually, in the month of April, by the clerks of the several districts, to the State Superintendent.

Chap. 369, Vol. 16.
Time for attendance upon institutes not to be deducted.

The time during which each teacher shall be in attendance upon the institute shall not be deducted from his or her period of service as teacher by the commissioners of any district.

ARTICLE XI.

ASSESSMENTS.

R. C. Chap 42, Sec. 12.
Assessment, how made.
Polls.

It shall be the duty of the school committees of the several school districts to make assessment lists for their respective districts. Such lists shall consist of the rates of persons of all the white male inhabitants of the district over twenty-one years old; of the rates of the

Chattels.

personal property of all the white inhabitants of the district; and of

Rental value of lands.

the clear rental value of all the assessable real estate within the district

Chap. 46, Vol. 15.

owned by white persons. The personal property of all white persons

Personal property liable to taxation for school purposes.

now subject to tax for school purposes in the school districts shall be liable to assessment and tax for school purposes in the school district

Shall be assessed only where actually located.

only in which it is actually located; and it shall be the duty of the

Duties of school committees relative thereto.

school committees of the several school districts within the limits of this State, making the assessment lists for their respective districts, to place thereon the rates of the personal property now subject to tax for school purposes in the school district in which it has an actual location only, irrespective of the residence of the owners thereof. The school committees of the several school districts within this State shall not take the rates of personal property from the assessment list of the hundred in which it stands assessed at the time, but shall fix the rates

Property to be viewed personally.

of personal property for their respective school districts upon personal view thereof, or other sufficient information of the owners or persons having control of the same. The said school committees, in making the assessment lists for their respective school districts, shall adopt and use as a guide the assessment list of the hundred in which their districts may be situated, so far as it may be practicable. The assessment list of each school district aforesaid, shall only include the personal

Proviso.

property actually located therein: *provided* that no property shall be assessed for school purposes, under the provisions of this act, which is exempted from taxation for county purposes. They shall assess the clear rental value beyond reprises of all the assessable real estate in the district, and make out a list of the names of the persons assessed in alphabetical order, the rates of persons,* and of personal property, number of acres or other description of real estate, and the clear rental value thereof. When the line between two districts crosses the lands of any person occupied in one body, the whole of such lands shall be assessed in the district where the dwelling-house is, and no part in the other : *provided* that any tenant residing on such lands, in an adjoining district, shall, at his election, communicated in writing to the school committee of such adjoining district, at any time prior to the completing of the assessment list, be only assessed, and have school privileges, in the district in which such tenant resides.

Lists of names of persons assessed.

When line between two districts crosses lands of any person.

Chap. 370, Vol. 16.

It shall be the duty of the school commissioners in each of the school districts of the State, annually, in the month of April, to assess and levy, without regard to any vote thereon, in each of their respective districts, that is to say: in each of the school districts in New Castle county, the sum of one hundred and fifty dollars; in each of the school districts of Kent county, the sum of one hundred and twenty-five dollars; and in each of the school districts in Sussex county, the sum of sixty dollars, to be applied to the support of the schools of their districts respectively.

Sec. 8 Chap. 369, Vol. 16.

Amount of tax to be levied without regard to vote thereon.

A copy of the assessment list shall be posted in some public and suitable place of the district for inspection ; and the committee shall, by advertisement in at least five public places in the district, give notice that said list is posted, and where; and of the day, hour and place (not less than five days thereafter), of their sitting to hear objections to it. Upon such hearing they shall make all just corrections, and add anything omitted, but they shall not alter a rate taken from the assessment list of a hundred [with regard to the rates of persons.] They may adjourn if necessary.

R. C. Chap. 42, Sec. 12.

Copy of assessment list to be posted.

Notice of it.

Notice of time and place of appeal.

Corrections of list.

The list, when settled, shall be conclusive, and shall stand until the next assessment in the district, when a new list shall be made for each school district.

R. C. Chap. 42, Sec. 12.

List when settled shall be conclusive.

---

*It appears that the commissioners of School District No. 53, in New Castle County, are authorized to increase the capitation or poll assessment in said district sufficient to raise the difference between $550 and $700, by Chapter 406, Volume 14, passed April 1st, 1873.

Proceedings of committee not to be questioned but for fraud.

The proceedings of the committee in making an assessment list shall not be questioned, except for fraud, or corruption.

Vol. 12, Chap. 296, Sec. 2.

School committee to revise the assessment of rental values annually.

The several school committees elected shall, annually, on oath or affirmation, revise and adjust the assessments of rental values in their respective districts, so as to make them bear a due proportion to each other, having respect to their productiveness to their several owners.

Vol 12, Chap. 296, Sec. 3.

Non-residents to be notified by clerk of district of time and place of appeal.

As soon as said assessments have been so adjusted, it shall be the duty of the clerks of the several districts to direct a letter to the address of each non-resident, whose rental valuation has been assessed in any district, stating the amount of his or her rental valuation in any of said districts, and the day and hour when the school committee will sit as a Court of Appeal to hear any objections that may be made to said assessment.

The following are the districts which are authorized to raise a sum of money in excess of the amount which each district is required to raise :

Chap. 552, Sec. 1. Vol. 11.

School District No. 3, in New Castle county, may raise, annually, by tax, $500 for the support of schools in said district.

Chap. 419, Vol. 11.

School District No. 19, in New Castle county, may raise, annually, by tax, $600 for the support of schools in said district.

Chap. 140, Vol. 13.

The Committee of School District No. 21, in New Castle county, are authorized, directed and empowered to mortgage the two-story brick school house belonging to said district and the lot or piece of ground appurtenant thereto for a sum not exceeding ($2000) two thousand dollars, payable in yearly installments of ($400) four hundred dollars each, on the first day of March in each year, together with lawful interest for the same. The said commissioners and their successors in office are authorized, directed and required to levy, yearly (in addition to the tax for carrying on the school directed to be levied at the stated meeting), the said sum of four hundred dollars, together with the amount necessary to pay the interest on said mortgage and the expenses of collecting said tax, and pay the same to the mortgagee, his heirs and assigns, as the same may become due and payable according to the terms of said mortgage.

Chap. 142, Vol. 13.

School District No. 53, in New Castle county, may raise, by taxation, yearly, $400 for the support of schools in said district.

Chaps. 427 and 428, Vol. 13.

School Districts Nos. 8 and 20, in New Castle county, each may raise, by taxation, annually, any amount not exceeding $600 for the support of the public schools therein.

Chaps. 429 and 430, Vol. 13.

School Districts Nos. 91 and 29, in New Castle county, each authorized to borrow a sum of money not exceeding $1500, on mortgage of the school house and ground appurtenant thereto, payable in three equal annual installments ; and the commissioners of said districts authorized to levy and collect, yearly, in addition to the tax for carrying on the school therein, such sum as shall be necessary to meet said annual payments.

School District No. 20½, in New Castle county, authorized to mortgage the school property therein on such conditions as the commissioners may consider most conducive to the interest of said district. Chap. 431, Vol. 13.

School District No. 78, in New Castle county, may raise, annually, by taxation, any amount not exceeding $1500 for the support of a free school in said district. Chap. 44, Vol. 14.

School District No. 67, in New Castle county, authorized to raise, by taxation, any amount not exceeding $600 for the support of free schools in said district. Chap. 45, Vol. 14.

United School District Nos. 11 and 81, in Kent county, may raise by taxation, annually, $500, in addition to the amount now authorized by law, for the support of a free school in said district. Chap. 47, Vol. 14.

School District No. 93, in New Castle county, may raise by taxation, annually, the sum of $600 for the support of the public school. Chap. 51, Vol. 14.

School District No. 40, in New Castle county, authorized to raise $1500 for the procurement of a lot of ground and the erection of a school house thereon. Chap. 395, Vol. 14.

School District No. 63, in New Castle county, authorized to borrow a sum not exceeding $2000 for the purpose of erecting a school house and furnishing the same. Chap. 396, Vol. 14.

Schools of the town of New Castle authorized to raise such sums as the Committee on Education shall direct, not to exceed $3000 annually. Chap. 397, Vol, 14.

United School District Nos. 23 and 75, in New Castle county, may raise by taxation, annually, any amount not exceeding $1500. Chap. 400, Vol. 14.

School District No. 91, in New Castle county, authorized to raise, yearly, for two consecutive years, $300 to liquidate the debt due on school house—1873. Chap. 401, Vol. 14.

School District No. 94, in New Castle county, authorized to borrow any sum of money not exceeding $2500 for the purpose of erecting and furnishing a new school house in said district—1873. Chap. 402, Vol. 14.

School District No. 21, in New Castle county, may raise, annually, by taxation, any sum not exceeding $1000 for the support of public schools. Chap. 403, Vol. 14.

School District No. 94, in New Castle county, may raise by taxation, annually, $500 for the support of public schools. Chap. 404, Vol. 14.

United School District Nos. 3 and 77, and United School District Nos. 5 and 107, in Kent county, may each raise by taxation, annually, any sum not exceeding $600, subject to the vote of the school voters therein. Chap. 405, Vol. 14.

School District No. 53, in New Castle county, may raise by taxation, annually, $700 for the support of the school, and the commissioners empowered to increase the capitation tax. Chap. 406, Vol. 14.

School District No. 72, in Sussex county, may raise, annually, by taxation $150 in lieu of the amount required to be raised by law for support of a free school; and may raise any sum not exceeding $400, if the school voters therein shall so determine. Chap. 43, Vol. 15.

United School District Nos. 39 and 41, may raise, annually, by taxation $1000 for the support of a graded school. Chap. 44, Vol. 15.

School District No. 91, in Sussex county, may raise by taxation, annually, $100 for school purposes. Chap. 37, Vol. 16.

ARTICLE XII.

LEVY AND COLLECTION OF TAXES.

R. C. Chap. 42, Sec. 13.
Chap. 354, Vol. 16.
Taxes, how levied.

Upon the completion of the assessment and levy of the school tax in the school districts in this State by the respective school committees, provided for in Article XI, they shall determine the rate on every hundred dollars of the amount of the assessment list required to raise the sum levied with ten per centum added thereto for delinquencies and costs of collection. After determining the rate as aforesaid, it shall and may be lawful for said school committees to accept and receive the tax of each and every person liable to pay the same who shall tender the payment thereof before the tenth day of May in the year in which said tax shall be levied, and the committees shall allow to every person so paying their tax within said time an abatement of eight per cent. upon said tax.

Chap. 354, Vol. 16.

Delivery of duplicate of uncollected taxes to collector.

It shall be the duty of the school committee in the several school districts aforesaid, on the tenth day of May in each year, or as soon thereafter as practicable, to execute and deliver their warrant, with duplicate of the uncollected assessment list, to a collector specially appointed by said school committee, or to the collector of county taxes for the hundred in which such school district may be situated, and the said collector shall be and he is hereby required to accept the same

Powers of collector.
R. C. Chap. 42, Sec. 13.

and collect the taxes thereon assessed. To execute the said warrant the said collector shall proceed in the manner and have all powers of a collector of county rates.

The warrant may be in this form :

Form of warrant.

————— *County, School District No.* ——— *ss.*

The State of Delaware :   To the Collector of ———

We command you to collect from the respective persons named in the annexed duplicate, the rate of ——— *on every hundred dollars of the amount with which they respectively stand assessed, according to said duplicate ; and if either of said persons shall not, in ten days after demand, pay the sum which you are required to collect from him, you are authorized to proceed in the manner and use all the means provided by law for the collection of county rates.   Given under the hands and seals of the subscribers, members of the school committee of the district aforesaid, the* ——— *day of* ———, *A. D. 18*—.

If any collector of a hundred refuse to receive and execute a warrant, directed to the collector of said hundred, according to this section, he shall forfeit and pay to the school district, whose school committeé issued such warrant, the sum of fifty dollars. The executor or administrator of a collector may execute the warrant, and shall have all his powers. The oath of the collector, or of his executor, or administrator, shall be competent evidence of the demand; and no demand shall be necessary in case of a non-resident of the district.

R. C. Chap. 42. Sec. 13.

Penalty for neglecting or refusing by hundred collector to serve

Executors or administrators of collector.

Demand, how proved—on non-resident not necessary.

In addition to the powers now possessed by school tax collectors in this State, it shall and may be lawful for any such collector, after demand made by him for the payment of the tax assessed against any inhabitant of the school district for which he is collector, and the failure of said taxable to pay the same on said demand, to give written notice to any person residing in the county wherein said district is located whom he may suppose to have in his possession any goods or chattels, rights or credits, moneys or wages, belonging or owing to said taxable, stating the amount of taxes due from said delinquent taxable; and if the person so served with notice shall fail to deliver up such goods and chattels, or to pay so much money or wages in his possession as shall satisfy said school tax due from said delinquent, said collector may proceed, by suit in the name of the school commissioners of the district, before any Justice of the Peace in and for said county, against any person so notified, as aforesaid, and recover against him, her, or them, a judgment for the amount of said tax of said delinquent, with costs, or for so much of said tax as may be equal to the value of the goods and chattels, rights and credits, moneys and wages in his, her, or their hands or possession at the time of service of said notice, or at any time between then and the rendition of said judgment. The process, mode of trial, right of appeal, and form of proceeding shall be as prescribed in Chapter 99 of the Revised Statutes of this State. The oath of the collector shall be sufficient evidence of the demand and refusal of the aforesaid [tax] and of service of said notice.

Chap. 351, Vol. 16.

Power of school tax collector to attach effects of taxables.

Right to sue persons failing to respond to notice

Mode of trial, &c.

If a person, liable to pay a rate, removes from the district, or dies without payment, it shall be deemed a debt due to the collector, and may be recovered by suit before a Justice of the Peace.

R. C. Chap. 42, Sec. 13.

Persons removing, &c.

R. C. Chap. 42,
Sec. 14.

Collector to pay
over in thirty
days.
Delinquencies,
fees, &c.

Liability of
collector.

The collector shall, within thirty days after receiving the warrant, pay to the school committee the amount which he is required to collect, deducting delinquencies to be allowed by them, and his fees, at the rate of ten per cent. on the sum collected when it does not exceed fifty dollars, and eight per cent. when it exceeds that sum ; and every collector of a hundred, and his sureties, by virtue of his official bond, shall be liable thereon for every failure of duty and default in the premises; which bond shall be proceeded on at the instance of the school committee of the district aforesaid.

R. C. Chap. 42,
Sec. 15.
Penalty for
neglect.
Suits, &c., to be
brought.

If any collector shall neglect to pay to a school committee the money collected by him on their warrant, and due, such committee may, if the amount does not exceed one hundred dollars, sue him, in their own names, before a Justice of the Peace, and recover the same.

Chap. 16, Sec. 1,
Vol. 13.

Action of debt
may be brought
before Justice of
the Peace against
school committee
or survivors for
money due
district.

Where it appears, upon settlement by the school committee of a district, that there is due from said committee to the district, for money actually received by said committee, any sum whatever, an action of debt may be brought in the name of the district, or against the said committee, or the survivor or survivors of them, in their individual names, for recovery of the same, as also for the penalty now provided by law ; and judgment thereon shall be given as in other cases, and may be executed accordingly ; such action, no matter what the sum demanded be, may be brought before a Justice of the Peace, and shall be proceeded in as other actions within their jurisdiction are.

ARTICLE XIII.

SCHOOL FUND.

R. C. Chap. 42,
Sec. 2.

Sources of Free
School fund.

The clear income of the School Fund of this State is hereby appropriated and apportioned among the school districts as follows : Of the investments made of the surplus revenue fund—the dividends on the investment in five thousand shares of Farmers' Bank stock, made under act of February 21, 1837 ; and the interest on one hundred and thirty-one thousand seven hundred and fifty dollars of the bond for one hundred and fifty-six thousand seven hundred and fifty dollars of the State of Delaware to the School Fund of said State, at six per cent. interest, issued under the provisions of Chapter 324, Volume 16; and the interest on the sum of five thousand dollars, advanced to the

County of Sussex under the act of February 17, 1837, shall be divided, Distribution. as they fall due, among the counties equally; and the Trustee of the School Fund shall so distribute these dividends and interest among the counties, (taking into consideration the said loan of five thousand dollars made to the County of Sussex,) as that each county shall receive an equal share of the interest and benefit derived from the said surplus revenue fund, invested as aforesaid; and shall apportion and distribute the same among the school districts of said counties respectively, in the same manner as other income of the school fund, [*pro-* Ch. 486, Vol. 15. *vided* that the interest on the said sum of $5,000 advanced to the County of Sussex, as aforesaid, shall be added to and form a part of that proportion of the dividend and income from the said school fund belonging to said County of Sussex;] and all the clear dividends or profits, to be declared, or accrue, upon any other bank stock, or other securities, or property, belonging to said fund, together with the clear sum arising from fees for marriage and tavern licenses, and any other income of said fund, or money directed by law to be paid to the trustee of said fund for distribution, shall be apportioned among the several counties according to their white population, as ascertained by the census of eighteen hundred and thirty.

The Trustee of the School Fund, in the apportionment of the share Chap. 442, Sec. 1, Vol. 11. of each of the counties of this State of the income of the School Fund Distribution of School Fund of among the school districts of the several counties in August, annually, each county equally among shall distribute and apportion the same equally among all the districts all the districts of the county. in the respective counties, without regard to the fact whether the said districts are original or subdivided, and so that each district in the same county, whether original or subdivided, shall receive the same sum or share, except that in the apportionment of the share of New Castle county, among the several districts thereof, the said trustee shall set apart one-seventh part thereof, and shall distribute the same among Exception as to the City of the districts contained within the limits of the City of Wilmington, Wilmington. and the residue among the remaining districts equally. [Under the provisions of Chapter 446, Volume 13, and Chapter 55, Volume 15, the Trustee of the School Fund is directed to pay over the dividends accruing from the distribution of the School Fund belonging to Districts Nos. 3 and 19 to the Board of Public Education of the City of

United districts entitled to share of the several districts of which composed.

Wilmington.] United districts shall be entitled to the several shares of the districts of which they are composed.

R. C. Chap. 42, Sec. 2.

He shall keep an account with each district, and enter its portion to its credit.

He shall, annually, deduct thirty dollars from the share of each $30 to be deduct- county, to pay for printing for the school convention for such county, ed from each county to defray such payment to be made by him on the order of the president of such expenses of county conven- convention. If the said sum be not so drawn, it, or any balance of tion. it, shall be carried to the share of the county for the next year.

ARTICLE XIV.

DRAFTS ON THE SCHOOL FUND.

R. C. Chap. 42, Sec. 16.

Orders on School Fund, how made

Vouchers paid by the Trustee of School Fund.

Whenever the school voters in any school district shall, by subscription, or tax, raise in any year twenty-five dollars, the school committee may draw an order on the Trustee of the School Fund for such district's share of the proceeds thereof. Such order, accompanied by a certificate that the committee has actually received that amount, shall be accepted and paid by the said trustee to the extent of any sum that may stand to the credit of the district when the order is presented ; and any money that shall be placed to its credit during that year of the account, shall be applicable to the balance.

R. C. Chap. 42, Sec. 17.

Commencement of school year.

Arrears, how drawn.

Forfeiture of district's share of fund.

The year of accounts with school districts shall commence on the first day of August; and at the end of every such year the accounts of all the districts shall be closed. An order drawn on the faith of money raised in one year, shall not be paid out of sums credited to the district in any other year ; but any money remaining to the credit of a district at the end of the year, may be drawn by the committee on their order and certificate that the said district has raised and paid to them a sum equal to what would have been necessary to draw the same in the year when it was credited to the district; and if it be not so drawn within three years, it shall be forfeited, and shall be carried to the county's portion of the school fund, divisible among all the districts thereof, the next year.

R. C. Chap. 42, Sec. 17.

The Trustee of the School Fund shall certify the date of each order, and the sum paid thereon, and the amount stated in the certificate to

have been raised in, the district, to the Auditor of Accounts, who shall Trustee shall certify payments to Auditor.
charge the committee with that amount on settlement.

If any person shall make a fraudulent certificate for the purpose of R. C. Chap. 42, Sec. 18.
drawing money from the Trustee of the Fund aforesaid, he shall be Penalty for drawing school money by fraud-ulent certificate.
deemed guilty of a misdemeanor, and fined double the amount of such
certificate.

ARTICLE XV.

SETTLEMENT OF SCHOOL COMMITTEES WITH THE AUDITOR.

The Auditor shall settle the accounts of the school committees who R. C. Chap. 42, Sec. 19.
have drawn money as aforesaid. For this purpose every such commit- Settlement of school committee with Auditor.
tee shall, under penalty of forfeiting to the district twenty five dollars
for neglect, appear with their accounts and vouchers before him, when When made.
he shall attend in their county to settle the account of the County Notice to com-mittee by Auditor.
Treasurer and others, whereof he shall give notice. He may compel Penalty for neg-lect by com-mittee.
them, by attachment, to appear and settle.

The settlement shall show how long a school was kept in the district, What settlement must show.
the compensation of the teacher, and the number of scholars, the sum
raised. and whether by tax or voluntary contribution; the sum drawn,
and the sum expended; all of which shall be stated in the Auditor's Auditor's report, what to state.
report to the General Assembly.

For the purpose of information with respect to the state of the R. C. Chap. 42, Sec. 19.
schools, the Auditor shall prescribe forms of returns of school com- Forms to be fur-nished to school
mittees, containing such questions as he shall propound, for collecting committee by Auditor.
the statistics of all the free schools in the State. He may require Returns of com-mittee must cor-
returns according to such forms, fully answering the questions pro- respond with forms.
pounded, so far as within the power of the school committees. He
may refuse to settle the account of the school committee until the Failure to settle according to such
proper return be made; and if, in consequence, settlement of any forms, penalty.
account shall not be made during his attendance for that purpose, the
school committee shall incur the forfeiture by this article provided;
and there shall be the same liabilities and consequences as if they had
failed to appear.

If the committee fail to appear and settle with the Auditor, or if, on Default of com-mittees.
such settlement it appear that they have misapplied, or do not account

5

Auditor to make
known facts to
chairman, &c. of
stated meeting. for the money received by them, or with which they are chargeable, the Auditor shall make known the facts by letter, addressed to the chairman and secretary of the last stated meeting.

ARTICLE XVI.

SOURCES OF THE SCHOOL FUND.

R. C. Chap. 40,
p. 197-8.
School Fund. All money appropriated to, or invested for, "the fund for establishing schools in the State of Delaware," shall belong to "the school fund of the State of Delaware."

Trustee.

Powers. The State Treasurer for the time being shall be Trustee of this fund, with power to receive, sue for, and recover any money, or property bequeathed, given, or belonging to said fund; to vote as holder of any stocks belonging to said fund; to lease any real estate devised, given, or belonging thereto, for terms not exceeding three years, and to distrain for and collect the rents thereon accruing, and to improve and manage such estate, as may be proper.

Donations, ap-
plication of. The public faith is solemnly pledged for the faithful appropriation of all bequests, or gifts, to said fund, towards the establishment and support of schools for instruction in reading and writing, arithmetic, grammar, and such other branches of knowledge as belong to a good English education. No part of said fund shall be applied to any academy, college, or university.

Settlements to be
published. The Trustee of the School Fund shall, annually, upon settling his account with a committee of the legislature, publish the particulars of

Patrons' names. such settlement, and shall mention the name of any person who has made a gift, or bequest, to said fund, with the amount, or value thereof.

R. C. Chap. 40,
Sec. 4.
Sec. 20, Chapter
117, Vol. 13.
Sources of reve-
nue. The proceeds of marriage and tavern licenses; *one-fourth of all the money arising from the licenses for auctioneering; foreign life insurance agency; foreign fire insurance agency; vending of goods, wares, and merchandise by samples; keeping or traveling jacks or stallions; keeping eating-houses; taking photographs; acting as brokers; real estate agency; exhibiting circuses; practising jugglery; selling vinous, spiritous, or malt liquors; and also one-fourth of the money arising from fees on commissions issued to Prothonotaries, Clerks of the Peace, Registers of Wills, Recorders of Deeds, Clerks of the Orphans'*

Court, and Sheriffs ; and all other money or property given, appropriated, or belonging to said fund, are appropriated and dedicated to the purpose of public education in the State of Delaware : *provided,* Proviso that in case of a deficiency of the State funds, it shall be lawful for the State Treasurer to apply any part of the proceeds of marriage and tavern licenses to the payment of the salaries of the judiciary, and to deduct the same from the gross amount of the revenue for distribution among the school districts.

The following are the present investments and subjects of general Investments. appropriation belonging to the school fund, viz :

1. 5,000 shares of the increased stock of the Farmers' Bank, on which $36 per share have been paid ; .

2. $156,750 invested in a bond of the State of Delaware to the School Fund of said State, under Chapter 324, Volume 16 ; which includes the proceeds of the sale of the certificates of loan to the Philadelphia, Wilmington and Baltimore Railroad Company, and the sum of $25,000 invested in stock of the New Castle and Wilmington Railroad Company, which has been paid.

3. Loan of $5,000 to the County of Sussex ;

4. 2,439 shares of Farmers' Bank stock, at $50 per share, held thus—1,904 at Dover, 295 at New Castle, 240 at Georgetown ;

5. 37 shares of the stock of the Bank of Delaware ;

6. 114 shares of the stock of the Bank of Smyrna ;

7. 127 shares of the Union Bank stock ;

8. 65 shares of stock in the United States Bank of Pennsylvania ;

9. Fees on marriage and tavern licenses ; *one-fourth of all the* Appropriations. *money arising from licenses for auctioneering ; foreign life insurance* Sec. 20, Chapter *agency ; foreign fire insurance agency ; vending of goods, wares, and* 117, Vol. 13. *merchandise, by samples ; keeping or traveling jacks or stallions ; keeping eating-houses ; taking photographs ; acting as brokers ; real estate agency ; exhibiting circuses ; practising jugglery ; selling vinous, spiritous, or malt liquors ; and also one-fourth of the money arising from fees on commissions issued to Prothonotaries, Clerks of the Peace, Registers of Wills, Recorders of Deeds, Clerks of the Orphans' Court, and Sheriffs.*

LAWS RELATING TO SCHOOLS FOR COLORED PERSONS.

The Levy Courts in the several counties of this State are authorized and required, annually, in the month of April, to lay and apportion a tax of thirty cents in the hundred dollars, and so *pro rata*, upon the assessments of the real and personal property and poll of colored persons, as they shall stand upon the assessment lists of the several hundreds, which shall be set apart as a separate and distinct fund for the support and maintenance of colored schools in this State. The warrant required to be issued to the collectors of the several hundreds shall include the taxes levied under this act. The said taxes shall be collected by the collectors aforesaid, by the same process as other taxes now are, and [they shall] pay over the same as hereinafter directed. ^{Section 1, Ch. 48, Vol. 15. Ch. 369, Vol. 15. Levy Courts to tax colored persons for support of their own schools. Tax rate. Separate fund. How collected.}

All moneys collected under this act shall be paid as other taxes to the County Treasurer in each county, which he shall keep as a separate fund, and which shall be paid by him to the Treasurer of the "Delaware Association for the Education of Colored People;" and at the time of each and every payment he shall furnish the association with a statement, showing the respective amounts received by him from the different hundreds of his county. The fund arising under the provisions of this act and paid to said association, shall be applied to the support and maintenance of colored schools throughout this State, and shall be distributed by said association as follows, to wit: The said association shall take the statement furnished by the County Treasurer and distribute to each hundred the amount paid to the Treasurer by each hundred, under the provisions of Section 1st of Chapter 48, Vol. 15. And in case there shall not be any school kept and maintained in any hundred during any year, the amount paid in from said hundred shall be retained and held by said association until a school or schools shall be organized and kept in each hundred, when it shall be applied toward the support of such school or schools. ^{Chap. 373, Vol. 16. Money collected for colored schools to be paid to County Treasurer. Distribution of money, by whom. Conditions.}

Treasurer of the Delaware Association for the education of the colored people to give bond.
> The treasurer of said association shall give bond to the State of Delaware for the penal sum of two thousand dollars, conditioned for the faithful application of the moneys received under this act.

Bond of county treasurer and county collectors liable.
> The official bond of the County Treasurer and county collectors to each county shall be liable for the moneys collected and received under this act.

Rate of commissions.
> The County Treasurer and collectors to each county shall be entitled to the same per cent. for the collection and application of the moneys collected and accounted for, under this act, as they are for the collection and application of county taxes.

Ch. 362, Vol. 16. Appropriation of money for colored schools.
> The sum of two thousand four hundred dollars is appropriated, annually, from the State Treasury, to be expended for the purpose of educating the colored children of this State. The money so appropriated

To whom paid.
> shall be paid by the State Treasurer to the Treasurer of the "Delaware Association for the Education of the Colored People," on or before the first day of October of each and every year, beginning with the year one thousand eight hundred and eighty-one.

Bond of the Treasurer of the Delaware Association.
> The said treasurer of the Delaware Association shall give bond to the State of Delaware, in the penal sum of five thousand dollars, conditioned for the faithful application of all moneys received hereunder,

By whom approved.
Report.
> said bond to be approved by the Secretary of State and recorded in his office. Said treasurer shall make an annual report of all the receipts and expenditures under this act to the State Auditor in October of each year.

Distribution of money appropriated.
> The said Delaware Association shall distribute said sum of money among the colored schools of the State : *provided* that no school shall be entitled to receive its pro rata share unless said association is reliably informed that it has remained open for at least three months during

Ch. 373, Vol. 16.
> the school year, with an average attendance of at least fifteen scholars;

Ch. 362, Vol. 16.
> *and provided further*, that the said sum of two thousand four hundred dollars shall be divided into three equal parts of eight hundred dollars each, one of said parts to be expended in New Castle County, one in

Ch. 373, Vol. 16.
> Kent County, and one in Sussex County, to be apportioned to and among the several schools in each county equally.

AN ACT to exempt certain persons from the operation of Chapter 48 of Volume 15 of the Laws of Delaware, and to enable them to establish schools for their children in Sussex County.

SECTION 1. *Be it enacted by the Senate and House of Representatives of the State of Delaware in General Assembly met, (two-thirds of each branch of the Legislature concurring)*: That Whittington Johnson, William A. Johnson, Samuel B. Norwood, George L. Norwood, Robert W. Norwood, Elisha Wright, Beturn Wright, Selema Wright, Nicholas Wright, James H. Kimmey, Robert Clark, Thomas H. Clark, Myers B. Clark, Isaac Harmon, John Harmon, James H. Clark, William R. Clark, Ann Johnson, Robert B. Johnson, John Thompson, Theodore Harmon, Stephen M. Norwood, John Harmon, Mitchell Harmon, Gardiner Drain, David P. Street, David R. Street, David Wright, George W. Clark, Elias C. Clark, William Clark, all of whom are residents of Indian River Hundred, and Sussex County, of this State, are hereby and shall be hereafter exempted and relieved from the operation and burdens of Chapter 48 of Volume 15 of the Laws of Delaware, entitled "An act to tax colored persons for the support of their own schools," and the said Chapter 48 of Volume 15 of the Laws of Delaware shall in no manner apply to them.

Names of persons exempt from taxation under Chapter 48, Vol. 15, Laws of Delaware.

SECTION 2. *Be it further enacted*, That the parties named in the first section, and their successors, are hereby incorporated and constituted a body politic under the name of "The Indian River School Districts for a certain class of Colored Persons," and in such name may, among other things, have a corporate seal, take and hold ground for two school houses, and the appurtenances and furniture, and for such purposes may take and hold, by devise, bequest, or donations, real and personal estate, not exceeding in clear annual income five hundred dollars, for the use of the schools in said districts, and may alien the same; may take bond from their collector; may prosecute actions upon it, and any action for injury done to any property of the district, in which action they shall recover double damages and costs; and also any action for a forfeiture or penalty due to the district. Any of the said actions may be brought before a Justice of the Peace, if

Name of corporation.

Seal.

Corporate powers.

the sum demanded do not exceed one hundred dollars, and he shall proceed as in other demands of a like amount. The said district shall not possess any corporate powers or franchises other than those hereby expressly given it,

Mode of acquir-
ing membership.

SECTION 3. *Be it further enacted*, That any one may hereafter be made a member of this corporation by a two-thirds vote of those present at any stated meeting thereof, upon his posting, thirty days before said stated meeting, written notice of his application for mem-

Proviso.

bership on the front door of each school house : *provided* that no one shall be a member of this corporation who does not belong to the class of colored persons to which those mentioned in section one belong, is not above the age of twenty-one years, a citizen of this State, and a resident of said Indian River Hundred.

Division of
corporation.
Names of
districts.

SECTION 4. *Be it further enacted*, That the said corporation shall be divided into two sub-districts, called respectively " Warwick District" and " Hollyville District." The limits of said sub-districts shall be defined by five members of the corporation, to be selected by ballot at the first meeting of the corporation. They shall make report

Record of
districts.

of their proceedings to the corporation, and the same shall be recorded in its records; but said limits may, in like manner, be at any time changed; the five members only to be appointed at a stated annual meeting.

Time of
meeting.

SECTION 5. *Be it further enacted*, That the persons named in section one of this act shall meet on the first Saturday of April next, at two o'clock in the afternoon, at some place to be selected by a majority, and shall proceed, after selecting a chairman and secretary,

Voting.

to elect, by ballot, two school committees, one for each of said sub-

School
committees.

districts. Such school committees shall consist of a clerk and two commissioners, and shall be elected for the term of three years. They

Amount of
money raised.

shall also resolve, by a majority vote, what sum shall be raised for the purpose of purchasing a lot of ground and erecting thereon a school house in each of said sub-districts, provided said sum shall not exceed the sum of four hundred dollars; and shall also resolve, by a like vote, what sum shall be raised for the purpose of supporting the said two schools for the ensuing year, provided said sum shall not exceed the sum of two hundred dollars.

Section 6. *Be it further enacted,* That the members of said cor- Stated meeting.
poration shall have a stated meeting every year, on the first Saturday
of April, at two o'clock in the afternoon. Such meeting shall be held
at the Warwick school house, and Hollyville school house, in the Place of meeting.
alternate years, and shall be kept open at least one hour. Every
member who has paid his school tax for the preceding year shall have a Qualification of voters.
right to vote. One-third of the members of the corporation shall
constitute a quorum, and may proceed to business. They may appoint Quorum.
a secretary and chairman, and shall resolve, by a majority vote, what Officers.
sum shall be raised for the support of said two schools, provided that Amount of money to be
said sum shall not exceed, in any one year, the sum of two hundred raised.
dollars in the aggregate. They shall also elect a school committee, as
aforesaid, for the term of three years, whenever the terms have expired ;
and shall have the power to fill any vacancies by electing some one to Vacancies.
serve for the residue of the term. They shall also, at said stated
meeting, elect, by ballot, five members who shall then and there proceed to apportion to each member of the corporation his or her share Apportionment of tax.
or portion of the sum to be raised during the ensuing year for school
purposes as aforesaid, and shall make report of the same to the said
meeting. Any member of the corporation who is dissatisfied with the
report may appeal to the meeting, stating his grounds, and the matter Appeal.
shall be then and there decided by a majority vote. When said report
has been adopted by a majority vote, it shall be final and conclusive
upon all parties. They shall also, at said meeting, elect a collector, to Collector.
whom they shall give a proper warrant to collect the sum aforesaid
from the parties upon whom it is assessed, and who shall give bond in Bond.
the penal sum of four hundred dollars for the proper performance of
his duties. His oath shall be proof of a demand, and if a member Proof of demand
does not pay the amount apportioned to him for ten days after the
demand, the collector may bring suit therefor before a justice of the Suit for taxes.
peace. The collector for the past year shall, at said stated meeting,
render an account thereto, which shall be at once examined by a committee of three, to be appointed by the chairman.

Section 7. *Be it further enacted,* That the school committee of
each sub-district shall select the teachers for their respective schools, Teachers.
but the stated annual meeting shall determine how many months the School year.
school shall be open, and how much money shall be apportioned to

6

Apportionment of funds.

each sub-district from the aggregate sum to be raised for the year.

Who may attend the schools.

Each school shall be open to all the children between the ages of seven and twenty-one of those members who have duly paid to the collector of the preceding year the sum with which they were charged.

Withdrawal from membership.

SECTION 8. *Be it further enacted*, That any member who has paid all the sums with which he is charged, as aforesaid, may withdraw from membership in said corporation by giving notice, at the annual stated meeting, of his intention so to do : *provided, however*, that he shall immediately thereupon become again liable to the provisions of the said Chapter 48 of Volume 15 of the Laws of Delaware.

Passed at Dover, March 10, 1881.

Ch. 371, Vol. 16.

A SUPPLEMENT to the act entitled "An act to exempt certain persons from the operation of Chapter 48 of Volume 15 of the Laws of Delaware, and to enable them to establish schools for their children in Sussex County."

SECTION 1. *Be it enacted by the Senate and House of Representatives of the State of Delaware in General Assembly met :* That the

Colored schools of Sussex county to receive a *pro rata* share of funds appropriated for that purpose.

colored schools which are organized and incorporated under and by virtue of the act entitled "An act to exempt certain persons from the operation of Chapter 48 of Volume 15 of the Laws of Delaware, and to enable them to establish schools for their children in Sussex County," passed at this present session of the General Assembly, shall be entitled to and shall receive from the "Delaware Association for the Education of the Colored People," a *pro rata* share of the sum of money authorized to be distributed among the colored schools of Sussex County, under and by virtue of the act entitled "An act to encourage the education of colored people," and of the supplement thereto, passed

Proviso.

at this present session of the General Assembly : *provided* that the said schools shall not be entitled to receive their *pro rata* share of said sum unless said association is reliably informed that the said schools have remained open for at least three months during the school year, with an average attendance of twenty scholars, and have raised by taxation, under the law to which this is a supplement, at least the sum of twenty-five dollars for each of said schools during the preceding

When to take effect.

year : *provided, however*, that these provisions shall not take effect until the year of our Lord one thousand eight hundred and eighty-two.

Passed at Dover, April 8, 1881.

APPENDIX.

FORMATION OF ADDITIONAL DISTRICTS.

Art. IV, *et seq.*
Ch. 442, Vol. 11.

FORM OF PETITION.

To the Levy Court of . . . . . *County,*

at its . . . . *Session for* . . . . *18* . . :

Petition to lay out an additional district.

The undersigned, being owners or holders of real estate in School District No. . . , (or in School Districts Nos. . . . ,) in Kent County, respectfully represent, that an additional district may be formed from the district (or districts) aforesaid.

[*The reason why the new district is desired may here be inserted.*]

Your petitioners therefore pray the Court to appoint three judicious and impartial persons residing in said county, and without the limits of the said district (or districts) to go to the said district (or districts) and inquire concerning the propriety of laying out an additional district therefrom according to the provisions of the law in such case made and provided. And they will ever pray, &c.

(Signed here by petitioners.)

(Date.)

Although nothing is said in the act providing for the formation of an additional district in regard to giving notice of any proceedings preliminary to the application for that purpose to the Levy Court, yet it would seem eminently proper and necessary that due notice thereof should be given, stating the time when the petition would be presented to the Levy Court, the alterations proposed to be made, and the reasons therefor.

Notice of presentation of petition.

Possibly such notice may be required by implication of law arising from construction of the third paragraph of Article IV, the Legislature considering the language and spirit of that article applicable to the alteration in districts resulting from the formation of an additional district. The public convenience and the interest of the schools very evidently require that the Court should have authority to exercise discretionary power in the appointment of commissioners for laying out such districts.

It is also suggested, whether due notice should not be given, stating the time when the commissioners will go to the district or districts to

Notice of meeting of commissioners to lay out new district.

inquire concerning the propriety of laying out the additional district, and the place where they will meet to make the inquiry, in order that they may be fully and fairly informed upon the subject. Much injury is doubtless liable frequently to arise to schools from the facility with which new districts may be formed, and the impracticability of representing to the commissioners the sentiments of the whole district without such notice. There are other, and often more important matters of consideration, in laying out additional districts, and the consequent division of original ones, than the mere number of scholars left in the one or found in the other, which should guide both the court and the commissioners in their decisions in such cases.

Notice of first stated meeting. The persons appointed by the Levy Court to inquire concerning the propriety of laying out the additional district must give notice, in writing, ten days before holding the first regular stated meeting of school voters in the district to be created, of the time and place for holding such meeting, which notice must be posted in five of the most public places in the district.

Form. The form of notice of yearly meetings, with the word "additional" inserted before the word "school," in the second line, and signed by the persons required to give the notice, will be proper in this case.

Alterations of districts. The law referred to (act March 3, 1857,) and the foregoing petition and notice, apply to the forming of additional or new districts. Should other alterations be desired, the manner of proceeding therein, is to make application (by petition) to the Levy Court, which, with the concurrence of two-thirds of all the members, may make such alterations. In this case notice of the intended application, stating time when it will be made, and the alterations desired, must be given by advertisements, posted in four or more public places in each district to be affected by the change, twenty days before the application is made.

The following form of notice may be observed in such cases, to wit:

SCHOOL VOTERS.

Notice of application to alter district. Notice is hereby given that an application will be made to the Levy Court of . . . County, on . . . the . . . day of . . . 18 . . , during its ensuing . . . session, for [*here insert the desired alterations.*]

Dated the . . . day of . . . 18 . . .

(*Signed by the persons desiring the alterations.*)

YEARLY OR STATED MEETING.

The yearly, or stated meeting of the school voters in each district is to be held on the first Saturday in April, at two o'clock in the afternoon, at the school house of the district; or if there be no school house, at the place appointed by the Levy Court, until there shall be a school house. The meeting shall be kept open at least one hour.* *Article VI.*

The clerk of the school district, or if there be no clerk, the commissioners, or one of them, are required to give notice of this meeting by advertisements, under hand, of the day, hour and place, posted in five or more of the most public places of the district at least five days before the day of meeting. *Article IX, p. 22.*

FORM OF ADVERTISEMENT FOR YEARLY MEETING.

SCHOOL VOTERS.

Notice is hereby given that a stated meeting of the school voters in School District No. . . , [or United School Districts Nos. . .] in . . . County, will be held on Saturday, the . . . day of . . . next [*or instant, as the case may be,*] at two o'clock, afternoon, at . . in said district. Dated the . . day of . . 18 . . *Advertisement for stated meeting.*

A—— B——, *Clerk.*

When there is no clerk, the commissioners, or one of them, signs, thus:

C—— D——,
E—— F——, } *Com'rs.*

The acts of the meeting are not void although no notice be given; but the clerk or commissioner neglecting to give notice forfeits ten dollars. *Article IX, p. 22.*

OCCASIONAL MEETINGS.

Occasional meetings of the school voters in a district may be called by the clerk and commissioners, or any two of them. The call is by advertisements, under hand, of the business, and day, hour, and place, posted in five or more of the most public places of the district at least five days before the day of meeting. The business must be specified in the advertisements, and business not specified cannot be transacted. It must be at the place where the stated meetings are held. *Article VII.*

A vacancy in the school committee may be filled at an occasional meeting; in that case, in place of the words "to consider and determine," &c., in the annexed form, use the words: "*To elect a clerk* [*or a commissioner, as the case may be,*] *in lieu of*———." *Article VI, p. 20.*

---

* This provision as to time of holding meeting does not apply to School District No. 8, New Castle County, the hour for holding the meeting therein being from 4½ to 6 o'clock, P. M.

FORM OF ADVERTISEMENT FOR OCCASIONAL MEETING.

SCHOOL VOTERS.

Advertisement for an Occasional meeting. An occasional meeting of the school voters in School District No. . . , in . . County, is hereby called by the subscribers, to be held on . . . the . . . day of . . . next, [*or instant, as the case may be,*] at . . . o'cock in the . . . noon. at . . . in said district, to consider and determine [*here describe the business.*] Dated the . . . day of . . . , 18 . . .

E—— F——,
G—— H——, } School Committee.
I—— K——,

[*Two are sufficient.*]

ORDER OF BUSINESS IN YEARLY MEETING.

Article VI.   1. Appoint a chairman and a secretary.

Article IX, p. 22.   2. Let the school committee of the past year present their account, also their report, and the meeting appoint persons to settle the account; and as soon as the settlement is made, let it be reported to the meeting and entered on the minutes.

Article VI.   3. Elect by ballot a clerk or commissioner (as the case may be) in place of the one whose term expires on this day; or fill any other vacancy that may exist of clerk or commissioners. A majority of the ballots given is necessary to elect. No person but a school voter of the district can be elected.

R. C., page 215.   [By Sections 1 and 2, Chapter 138, Volume 13, Laws of the State of Delaware, the school voters were required, at the stated meetings held on the first Saturday in April, 1867, to elect by ballot, in the manner set forth in Section 3, Chapter 42, Revised Code, a clerk to serve for three years thereafter, and two commissioners, one for the term of two years, and another for the term of one year, or in each case till a successor be chosen; and at every annual meeting thereafter elect one member of the school committee to serve for the term of three years, &c.]

Article VI, p. 19.   4. Resolve what sum shall be raised in the district for a school house therein, or for a free school.

Article VI.   5. Vote by ballot respecting a tax.

This last vote must be taken at the yearly meeting or the substitute Article VI. therefor; it can be taken at no other time.

More than $400 cannot be raised by tax for a free school, exclusive Article VI. of the amount required to be raised without regard to any vote thereon; Article XI, p. 25. nor more than $500, by tax, for a school house, in one year, in any Article VI. district.*

The vote respecting a tax must be by ballot; it may be taken by writing "*For a Tax,*" on some slips of paper, and "*Against a Tax,*" on other slips; and each for a tax voting a slip "*For a Tax ;*" each against a tax, a slip "*Against a Tax.*"

It is important to attend to each of these items separately, and have the proper entry distinctly made in respect to it. The proceedings of a meeting have been a mere nullity in consequence of blending votes on several items. In respect to raising money, it is best to vote first what sum shall be raised, and enter the vote; and then vote concerning a tax, and enter this vote.

If two or more persons receive an equal number of votes for clerk, or commissioner, (as the case may be) there is no choice, and the meeting should vote again, and so on till one person receives the majority of all the votes.

The meeting is appointed at two o'clock, afternoon; [except District No. 8, New Castle County, which is appointed from 4½ to 6 o'clock, P. M.] After duly organizing the meeting and proceeding to vote for the officers to be elected, as soon as opportunity has been allowed to all the persons present to vote, the election *may* be closed after one hour, and the choice declared and entered. It is desirable to give time for the attendance of the school voters, but this is a matter of discretion; the hour appointed by law for their attendance is two o'clock, with the exception aforesaid.

---

*For a list of districts authorized to raise sums of money in excess of amount which each district is required to raise without regard to vote, see pages 26 and 27; also list of districts consolidated and incorporated, on pages 16 and 17.

CERTIFICATES.

Article VIII.   Two certificates of the proceedings of every meeting must be signed by the chairman and the secretary, and delivered, one to the clerk of the district, and the other to the Clerk of the Peace of the county. These certificates ought to be made and signed upon the spot, and delivered without delay.

Art. VIII, pages 20 and 21.   A chairman or secretary not doing his duty in this particular, within one month, is liable to a fine not exceeding $50; and the proceedings of the meeting shall be void.

FORM OF CERTIFICATE OF YEARLY MEETING.

Article VI.   At the stated meeting of the school voters in School District No. . . [or United School District Nos. . . .] in . . . County, held according to law on Saturday, the . . . day of . . . , 18 . . , at the district school house . . . in said district,
A—— B——, was appointed Chairman, and
C—— D——, Secretary.

Article IX, p. 22.   The account of the school committee of the past year, namely, —— ——, —— ——and —— ——, was laid before the meeting, and on motion, E—— F—— and G—— H—— were appointed to examine and settle the same. By a report, also, of said school committee, it appeared that there had been kept in the district by a male teacher a school for the period of . . . , the teacher's wages, the rate of . . . , and the highest number of scholars . . . . males, and . . . . females; and by a female teacher a school for the period of . . . ; the teacher's wages, the rate of . . . , the highest number of scholars, . . . males, and . . . females.

Article VI.   Upon a vote by ballot, K—— L—— was elected clerk, [*or commissioner, as the case may be,*] of the said district, he having a majority of votes.*

[*Here may be inserted the adoption of any resolution or statement of other business transacted which is not specified in this form.*]

Article VI.   *Resolved*, that the sum of . . . be raised in this district for a school house, [*or for a free school in said district.*]

The meeting voted by ballot respecting a tax for raising the above sum.

And there was a majority of votes for a tax, [*or against a tax, as the case may be.*]

Article IX, p. 22.   E—— F—— and G—— H——, appointed as above to examine and settle the account of the school committee of the past year, report, that they have examined and settled the same, and that upon said account there is a balance due to, [*or from, as the case may be,*] the district of . . .

Said report was adopted.

A—— *B*——, *Chairman.*

Attest: *C*—— *D*——, *Secretary.*

---

*The above should be substantially observed; but varied from so as to conform to facts.

FORM OF CERTIFICATE OF OCCASIONAL MEETINGS. Article VII.

Article VIII.

At an occasional meeting of the school voters in School District No. . . . . , in . . . . County, duly called by [*insert the name of the school committee calling the meeting,*] the school committee [*or two of the school committee, as the case may be,*] of said district, and held on . . . the . . . day of . . . 18 . . . , at [*here insert the place where the stated meetings are held,*] in said district,

   A—— B——, was appointed Chairman, and

   C—— D——, Secretary.

The chairman and secretary inquired respecting the advertisements of this Article VII. meeting, and found that advertisements of the business, and the day, hour and place of this meeting were posted on the . . . day of . . . , instant, [*or last, as the case may be,*] at [*here mention by a proper description every place in which an advertisement was posted,*] being five of the most public places of said district, and the business mentioned in said advertisements was [*here set forth the business as contained in the advertisements.*]

Upon a vote by ballot G—— H—— was chosen clerk in place of K—— L——, removed, [*or refusing to serve, or deceased, as the case may be.*]

Resolved—[*setting down any proceedings of the meeting, observing that no business can be transacted not mentioned in the advertisements.*]

        A—— B——, *Chairman.*

Attest :   C—— D——, *Secretary.*

ASSESSMENT AND COLLECTION OF TAX.

With respect to the assessment, the directions of the law are so plain, Article XI. that nothing need be added. All that is requisite, is to read and follow the directions in respect to making the list, giving notice, and hearing objections, and preserving the list.

If the line between districts crosses a farm or property held together, Article XI. the whole is to be assessed in the district where the dwelling house is ; provided that any tenant residing on such lands, in an adjoining district, shall, at his election, communicated in writing to the school committee of such adjoining district, at any time prior to the completing of the assessment list, be only assessed, and have school privileges, in the district in which such tenant resides.

The committee of any district shall issue to the collector of the Article XII. same, or to the collector of the hundred in which such district is situated, a warrant, with a duplicate of the uncollected assessment list, for collecting the tax, who is required to receive the same and pay over to the committee the amount due the district within thirty days. Page 30.

According to Section 13 of Chapter 42, Revised Code, the committee is required to issue to the collector of the district, or to the collector of any hundred in which such district, or any part thereof, is situate, a warrant, with a duplicate of the assessment, or any part thereof, annexed, for collecting said rate. This provision is omitted in Section 2 of Chapter 354, Volume 16, but does not appear to have been repealed by said Chapter 354, and is mentioned here for the information of school committees.

How tax may be collected when district, or property taxed, is in several hundreds
From the foregoing it appears that if the district is composed of parts of several hundreds, a warrant may be directed to the collector of each hundred, with a duplicate of that part of the list that is within his hundred. If a person is taxed in several hundreds, the whole tax may be on the duplicate annexed to either warrant, or the proper part divided to each.

Article XII.   FORM OF WARRANT TO A COLLECTOR OF A HUNDRED.

. . . . County, School District No. . . , ss.

The State of Delaware : To the Collector of . . . Hundred :

Form of warrant to collector.
We command you to collect from the respective persons named in the annexed duplicate the rate of . . . . on every hundred dollars of the amount with which they respectively stand assessed according to said duplicate, and the like rate on every less sum ; and if either of said persons shall not, in ten days after demand, pay the sum which you are required to collect of him or her, you are authorized to proceed in the manner and use all the means provided by law for the collection of county rates.

Given under the hands and seals of the subscribers, members of the school committee of the district aforesaid, the . . . . day of . . . . 18 . . .

A—— B——, [L. s.]
C—— D——, [L. s.]
E—— F——, [L. s.]

Any two of the school committee will be sufficient, although it is always best for all to join.

DRAFTS ON THE SCHOOL FUND.

Article XIV.   FORM OF CERTIFICATE OF MONEY RECEIVED, IN ORDER TO OBTAIN DIVIDEND.

We, the subscribers, members of the school committee of School District No. . . , in . . . . County, certify, that we have received, for the benefit of said
Article VI, p. 19. district, the sum of . . ,* raised [*by tax, or subscription, as the case may be.*]

Witness our hands the . . . day of . . . 18 . .

E—— F——.
G—— H——.
J—— K——.

[*Two will be sufficient.*]

Art. XII, p. 30.   *The collector is required to pay to the committee the sum he is required to collect, deducting delinquencies and fees, within thirty days after receiving his warrant.

ORDER ON TRUSTEE FOR DIVIDEND.

To the Trustee of the School Fund for Establishing Schools in the State of Delaware :

Sir: Pay to the order of . . . . , for the benefit of School District No . . . in . . . . County, the sum standing to the credit of said district under the laws concerning free schools.

Given under our hands as members of the school committee of said district the . . . . day of . . . . , 18 . .

E—— F——.
G—— H——.
J—— K——.

(Two of the committee will be sufficient.)

The committee, or two of them, having made and signed certificate and order in the forms above given, are to go to the Clerk of the Peace in their respective counties, and ask for a copy of the certificate of the proceedings of the last annual stated meeting of their district ; and having received it, take it, with their own certificate and order aforesaid, to the Farmers' Bank, where the school dividends for the county are made payable. Then, on delivery of these to the bank, the dividends for their districts will be paid them at any time after public notice has been given by the Trustee of the School Fund that said dividends are payable, which he does once every year.

MEETINGS CALLED BY CLERK OF PEACE.

FORM OF APPLICATION TO THE CLERK OF THE PEACE TO ADVERTISE A MEETING.

To the Clerk of the Peace for . . . . County:

The subscribers, school voters of School District No. . . . . . , in said county, request you to give notice according to law of the stated meeting of the school voters of said district on the first Saturday in April, 18 . , ; there being no clerk or commissioner of said school district to give this notice. Witness our hands the . . . . day of . . . . , 18 . . .

This application must be signed by at least five school voters of the district.

The clerk may observe the foregoing form of advertisement of yearly meeting, concluding with the words:

Given under my hand upon the application of five school voters of said district, (there being no clerk or commissioner to give this notice) the . . . day of . . . 18 . . .

——— ———, *Clerk of the Peace of . . . . County.*

This advertisement must be posted, as required for other stated meetings, in five or more public places in the district.

OATH OR AFFIRMATION.

Article VI, p. 20.   Each member of the committee must be sworn or affirmed to perform his duty with fidelity.

The oath or affirmation may be administered by a justice of the peace, or any other officer having general power to administer oaths.

FORM OF CERTIFICATE OF OATH OR AFFIRMATION OF CLERK OR COMMISSIONER.

. . . . *County*, *ss.* Be it remembered, that on this . . . . day of . . . . 18 . . . , A——— B———, Clerk, [*or commissioner,*] elect of School District No . . . , in . . . County, personally appeared before the subscriber, a Justice of the Peace in and for said county, and was duly sworn [*or affirmed,*] to perform his duty of clerk [*or commissioner,*] of said district with fidelity. In testimony whereof, I have hereunto set my hand the day and year aforesaid.

.   C——— D———, *Justice of the Peace.*

Under the law as it now exists, there will generally be but one member each year to be qualified as above; yet as vacancies in the committee may occur otherwise than by the regular expiration of the term, two or more members may be elected at the same time. Some of these may desire to be affirmed, others be willing to be sworn. In such cases the following form of certificate may be conveniently used, varying it to suit the particular case.

. . . *County*, *ss.* Be it remembered that on this . . . day of . . . 18 . . . personally appeared before the subscriber, a Justice of the Peace in and for . . . County, A——— B———, Clerk elect, and C——— D, Commissioner elect of School District Number . . . , in the county aforesaid, and the said A——— B———, Clerk elect, was duly affirmed, and the said C——— D———, Commissioner elect, was duly sworn, each respectively, to perform his duty as member of the committee of the district aforesaid with fidelity.

In testimony whereof, I have hereunto set my hand the day and year aforesaid.

C——— D———, *Justice of the Peace.*

The certificate should be filed by the clerk, and a copy thereof recorded with the minutes of the first meeting of the school committee held next after the annual or stated meeting of the school voters.

SECRETARY'S OFFICE,

Dover, January 6th, 1882.

In obedience to Section 10, Chapter 369, Volume 16, Laws of Delaware, I have codified and caused to be published all the laws of the State of Delaware relating to Free Schools of a general nature. Not deeming it within the scope of the authority vested by said section to publish in full all the laws of a special or local character relating to schools, I have, nevertheless, for the sake of convenience, given reference thereto.

In the preparation of this digest of the school laws, I have strictly adhered to the language of the text so far as it was consistent with the sense. On account of the numerous supplements and amendments, which have, from time to time, been made, I have been compelled, in order to preserve the connection as well as the sense, to omit some phrases and sentences and to supply others, to which attention is called by the use of brackets and asterisks. In order to aid persons desiring to consult the original text of the school laws, I have made copious references, on the margin, to the Revised Code, or to the volume of the laws of the State, where they may be found.

In order to facilitate the transaction of the business of the districts, I have appended various forms and instructions, with a general index to the laws and forms, referring both to the article and the page.

JAMES L. WOLCOTT,

Secretary of State.

INDEX.

NOTE.—The figures in the Index refer to the page and the Roman numerals to the article.

8